TUDOR LONDON
A. G. ROBERTSON

First published in 1968 by
Macdonald & Co. (Publishers) Ltd.
St. Giles House, 49 Poland Street London W.1

Made and printed in Great Britain by
Purnell & Sons Ltd., Paulton (Somerset) and London

Discovering London 4
TUDOR LONDON
A. G. ROBERTSON
Drawings by David Newton

MACDONALD : LONDON

Contents

Page

The Cover shows part of Hollar's panorama of the Thames which is now in the British Museum

Introduction

This book is the fourth in the *Discovering London* series
and covers one of the most dynamic periods in the history
of the city. For over a thousand years since its foundation by the Romans, the expansion of London had been
limited by its wall and by the great monasteries which
had grown up around it, owning most of the land.

But now, in the 16th century, the Dissolution of the
Monasteries released the city from the bonds which had
constricted its growth for so long, and also provided the
wealth and the space which led to a great new surge of
building. New Royal Palaces were built and old ones
rebuilt, while the rich noblemen, merchants, and favour-
ites of the court built themselves splendid town houses.
On a more humble level, the population of the city increased rapidly as people flocked to it, attracted by its
ever-increasing power and wealth.

Grateful acknowledgement is made to Mr. Brian
Spencer of the London Museum for his patience, assistance and advice in the preparation of this book.

A nobleman and his wife of the time of Henry VIII

Tudor London

The London that Henry Tudor, Earl of Richmond, came to in 1485 was a busy, bustling, boisterous city of 60,000 to 80,000 inhabitants whose nostrils were well accustomed to the prevailing smells of roughly 50 per cent incense and 50 per cent sewage.

The city wall was in a fair state of repair, as it had been substantially improved by Sir Ralph Joceline, the Lord Mayor between 1476 and 1477. He had carried out repairs to the north section between Aldersgate and Aldgate, and John Stow, the Tudor historian of London, tells us that in order to pay for the work:

He caused to be granted by the Common Council, that every citizen should pay every Sunday during his year 5d. And, above that, by his politic means caused diverse fellowship of worship to make every fellowship a certain length of the wall; and to encourage them he began with his own fellowship, which made the wall from All Hallows on the Wall unto Bishopsgate; and likewise other fellowships their parts.

Joceline was a Draper and the fellowships referred to were Guild Companies. What happened was that the Goldsmiths' Company repaired the section from Aldersgate to Cripplegate, the Skinners' from Aldgate towards Bishopsgate, and the Grocers' from All Hallows on the Wall toward the postern at Moorgate.

The ditch however was not in such good condition; in many places it had been built over and some of the surrounding areas had become gardens. All the building that had been going on near the ditch was the main cause of the trouble. For centuries the authorities had tried to stop people using the ditch as a convenient sewer and a dumping ground for rubbish, and in the City records of 6th June 1532 we read:

This day came the Wardens of the Curriers, and injunction was given to them in the name of all the company that they should forthwith cause all such filth, and other vyle things by them caste and layde in the Moredyche to the gret annoyance and perill of the King's liege people (i.e. to be removed) and also they had streightly in commandment that day nor noon of them from henceforth lay no more there.

In 1554 the condition of the ditch between Aldersgate and Newgate was so offensive that John Calthorpe, a Draper, paid for it to be covered over and at the end of Elizabeth's reign the City Corporation paid for the ditch between Aldgate and the Tower to be thoroughly cleaned out and converted into a sewer. This City ditch was first dug in 1213 but later excavations have proved that there was a Roman ditch there long before that date.

Originally the whole length of the ditch from the Tower to the Fleet was called 'Hondesdich' or 'Hundsditch'. In time this has changed to Houndsditch and we now have only one small section of road with that name covering the ditch running from Bishopsgate to Aldgate. This section was filled in and finally paved over in 1503. Stow suggests that the name came from the filth and dead dogs thrown into the ditch, and this may well be correct.

The site of the inner passage within the wall, with the wall itself and the broad ribbon of land occupied by the ditch, measured some 40 acres from east to west. This was common land and therefore it was up to the City Corporation how it was used. The Corporation still retains an interest in some of the houses on the site of the ditch: on many buildings you can still see the City coat of arms.

In 1485 the City was still essentially medieval. Its shape was dictated by its walls, but it was beginning to spread. Building was going on to the east through Ratcliff to Wapping, filling up Whitechapel and south of the river to Long Southwark and St. George's Church. In the 16th and 17th centuries the growth of London's population was alarming. Increased trade on the river meant that more sailors and dockers needed houses to live in, and this led to further development on the South Bank as far as Bermondsey and Rotherhithe.

In his survey of 1598 John Stow the historian tells us: *that not many years ago in Billingsgate ward were one and fifty households of strangers, whereof thirty of these households enhabited in the parish of St. Botolph, in the chief and principle houses, where they give £20 the year for a house lately letten for four marks (6/8d). The nearer they dwelled to the waterside the more they give for houses, and within 30 years before, there was not in the whole ward above three Netherlanders; at which time there was within the said parish levied, for the help of the poor, seven and thirty pounds by the year; but since they came so plentifully thither, there cannot be gathered above eleven pounds, for the strangers will not contribute to such charges as other citizens do.*

The flood of foreigners coming to live in England, was caused by religious persecution on the Continent. In many cases they brought the skills of their trade with them, but this also led to a certain resentment from Londoners. London was very crowded and within the area of the 'Liberties' of the City, the craft and victualling trades were strictly controlled by the Guild Companies and the City Corporation. Outside the walls of the City however the position was not nearly so well managed and it was easier for anyone to start in business on his own without being a member of the Guild. A thriving wool

9

weaving trade was going on within the City, when the new immigrants arrived, bringing with them silk weaving from the continent. Many of them settled permanently in the village of Shoreditch and in Spitalfields. A colony of Hat Makers came to Southwark and for the first time in this country the Flemings brought with them the idea of putting hops into beer. This meant it could be kept for some time without going flat or sour. Up till now

A suit of display armour made in 1590 for the Earl of Cumberland, Queen Elizabeth's champion

English beer had to be sold quickly and was generally brewed by the tavern-keeper's wife, often making a reputation for a local tavern. As soon as hops were widely used in the brewing business the brewery trade began to grow and stopped being a local business. Large breweries began delivering barrels to taverns and inns and became the wholesalers of the brewery trade.

Since medieval days, the City Corporation has appointed an 'Ale Conner' as part of their traditional control of the victualing trade. The 'Ale Conner' supposedly wore leather breeches and he discovered the quality of the ale by ordering two pints—one of which he spilt on a bench. Sitting on this puddle, he would then drink the second pint, and when it was finished he would see if his breeches had stuck to the bench. If they had, the ale was up to standard.

When Henry VII arrived in London he found that printing was already established in and around Westminster. Caxton had set up his press in the building next door to the Almonry, and after he died, his assistant Wynkyn-de-Worde moved the business to Fleet Street and so brought printing to that part of London. While foreign craftsmen were flocking to the areas outside the City there was also a substantial move into these areas from the City itself. This was because of simple economic pressures. London craftsmen, strictly controlled by their Guilds, made and sold their products within the City where there were strict rules against 'regrating' or wholesaling. Outside the City these rules did not always apply and in any case it was much more difficult for the Guilds to enforce them. Tradesmen who moved outside the reach of the Guilds found they could use methods which were frowned on in the City. Often their new methods were more efficient and so they became prosperous.

The Guild Companies in their turn fought hard for their chartered right to monopolise their trade, and on every occasion, such as when they had to apply for their charter to be renewed, they tried to increase their sphere of influence. Eventually the Guilds' powers stretched some 4 or 5 miles around London, and in one or two cases, in the time of Charles II, as far as 12 miles. However, by the middle of the 16th century they were beginning to lose control of the situation because of the sheer economic pressure of the growth of London and the demand for goods and services.

The influx of foreign Protestants naturally increased after the Reformation, but in Queen Elizabeth's reign there were many laws passed that tried to control the expansion of London, and throughout the 16th and 17th centuries the City authorities tried hard to prevent this growth. In 1564 for instance, they issued an order against taking in lodgers other than those who were relatives of the family. In 1580 a Royal Proclamation prohibited new buildings within 3 miles of the City gates and in 1596 the Privy Council drew the attention of the Middlesex Justices to:

the great number of dissolute loose and insolent people harboured in such and like noisome and disorderly houses as namely poor cottages and habitations of beggars and people without trade, stables, inns, ale houses, taverns, garden houses, converted to dwellings, ordinaries (cook houses) dicing houses, bowling allies and brothel houses.

All this helped to slow down the expansion of London, but the attractive possibilities of finding the streets of London paved with gold was soon to prove too much. Yet, even at the end of Elizabeth's reign, the 1593 map

A contemporary woodcut: whipping beggars through the streets

of London by John Norden shows that Spitalfields was still only sparsely built over. The Moor was still open fields, Kingsland and Hackney had yet to be absorbed into London, and Islington was still a village. There was little building beyond Gray's Inn and none north of the 'Way to Tyburn' (now Oxford Street). St. Giles was literally 'in the fields'. Building along Fleet Street and the Strand had extended to Charing Cross, and the area up to Westminster was occupied by Whitehall Palace, the Palace of Westminster, and the Abbey. Only Tothill Street had been fully built up. Yet, during the Tudor period, the population of the City had probably doubled.

In Tudor and Elizabethan times there was a wide division between the rich and the poor, and nowhere was this more apparent than in the way people lived. Trade was the driving force of the City's expansionism, and very few people living there were not involved in one way or another. This was the period when the Renaissance was beginning to spread its influence deep into the life of England. At the beginning of Henry VII's reign, the established rich merchants were about to learn the trick of making their capital work for them. Banks and banking had not yet arrived, except in the form of 'foundations' or some other fraternal interest in a Monastery, in which case the Monks would hold the traders' money in safekeeping. This even applied to Westminster Abbey where the King's Treasure was housed; but the scheme was not without problems. In 1303 even the King's Treasury was broken into and most of its contents were stolen.

Crosby Hall

A man of wealth could really only spend his money on two things: gold plate or fine clothes. The gold plate was displayed on his 'cupboard', the Elizabethan equivalent of the present-day sideboard. Such displays, as well as the accommodation for guests invited to view them on proper occasions, demanded a fine house. There were a number of these in London at the beginning of the period and building increased throughout Elizabethan times, mostly inside the City. Crosby Hall, which stood on the east side of Bishopsgate on the site which is now covered by Crosby Square and many of the surrounding buildings, is a fine example. It was first built in 1466 by Sir John Crosby, a Warden of the Grocers' Company and a member of the Woolmen's Company. He was a soldier as well as a businessman and had a very large staff, which of course included the usual number of apprentices and clerks, all of whom lived on the premises. He is buried in St. Helen's Church which stands almost next door.

The house had a frontage of 240 feet and went back from Bishopsgate Street for about 300 feet. It consisted of a large banqueting hall, a smaller dining parlour, a

A tudor 'cupboard' used for displaying gold plate

chapel, state apartments, a nobleman's lodging, butler's and purser's lodgings, porter's quarters, great kitchens, brew house, bake house, larders, and stables together with court houses and various outhouses. There was also an extensive garden.

Sir John died in 1475 and in 1483 Richard, Earl of Gloucester, moved into Crosby Hall—but only for a short time. Shakespeare mentions the hall in *Richard III* on three occasions but as the dates concerned do not coincide with its known history it would appear that this is artistic licence on Shakespeare's part. The Hall then went through several hands and eventually, in 1523, Sir Thomas Moore took the lease. In 1524 he sold the remains of the lease and we hear of a succession of owners including a Sir John Spencer in 1594. He was known as 'Rich Spencer' and lived at Canonbury Tower, Islington, which had been the 'country' home of the Priors of St. Bartholomew's. Spencer, like Sir John Crosby, was buried in St. Helen's Church. The house then came into the hands of William Compton, later Earl of Northampton, who had greatly annoyed Spencer by marrying his daughter.

As the story is told, 'Rich Spencer' would not countenance Compton's suit, so the lovers eloped. They managed this by Compton disguising himself as Spencer's baker. While he was making a delivery of bread, he met Spencer, who tipped him for making such an early delivery, not realising that Compton was carrying off his daughter in the bread basket. Later, when Spencer realised what had happened, he said that would be the 'last penny' Compton would ever receive from him, and proceeded to disinherit his daughter.

Some time later, Queen Elizabeth, who had heard the story, invited Spencer to stand as Godfather to a child she was interested in. Spencer could not refuse and as a gesture to the Queen said 'Now I have no child of my own I will leave my money to my Godchild'. It was at

15

this point Queen Elizabeth revealed that the Godchild was actually Spencer's own grandchild.

Shortly before the First World War, a proposal was made to demolish the building, but a restoration committee eventually managed to push through an alternative plan; the hall was taken down, moved to Chelsea where it was re-erected and is still in existence. It is now occupied by the British Federation of University Women, and is open to the public. You will find it just west of Chelsea Old Church on the Embankment. Crosby Hall is one of the few examples of Elizabethan building still in existence, although portions of others can be seen in various exhibitions and museums including the Victoria and Albert Museum.

The following list will give some idea of the furnishing of a prosperous merchant's house in Billingsgate. This particular house belonged to a merchant, John Porth, who died in 1525 leaving, among other things, numerous benches, cupboards and 'turned' chairs (one made in Spain), backgammon tables, several carpets, 50 yards of 'hanging' material, a four branch chandelier, half a dozen pictures, cushions, bedsteads, down pillows, feather beds, bolsters, and blankets. Chests full of materials and sleeves and clothes undergoing alteration and remaking, some in cloth of silver or embroidered with 'damaske golde'. Black, tawny, violet, and crimson gowns, some furred with mink or squirrel, riding coats and doublets.

Kitchen utensils included brass pots, frying pans, trivets, tableclothes, and abundant supplies of linen. Plate and jewels in gold and silver gilt included, chased and enriched, salt cellars, mazers, standing cups and goblets, rings, buckles, pendants, and girdles.

All this furnished a house which probably included a hall, parlour, four or five bedrooms and chambers, a kitchen and buttery, the shop and counting house, and sundry garrets and stores.

Most Elizabethan houses had little in the way of comfort, and were usually very draughty. They often had no glazed windows and lighting was most elementary. Elizabethans warmed themselves at blindingly smoky fires. Most houses were wooden, some were even pre-fabricated, and they were very poorly furnished. The poorer people lived most of their working time out of doors, rising at sunrise and going to bed at sunset; and trading in the streets for their living. Often they slept over or under their workshops.

One of the problems throughout the period, and indeed well on into the last century, was sanitation. Houses were generally built over their own, or somebody else's, cesspit. This had to be emptied, usually at night, by men who were sometimes known as 'Gong Farmers'. The luckiest people lived near a river or by the City ditch—their privy was built out over these convenient open sewers. Household rubbish was supposed to be left in the street for the 'rakers', who called periodically to collect it at night. They carried it off to the City dumps which were on the banks of the Walbrook, the Fleet, or the Thames. The centre of the road became a gully into which all rubbish would eventually find its way, even though it was against the City Ordinances for any of the bigger waste to be thrown into the road. Certainly most liquids found their way there. People who lived near a water conduit or who had a supply of water were ordered at certain periods to flush the gullies in order to clear them, but if large pieces of rubbish had found their way into the gullies these rapidly became blocked and the filthy water was soon washing into the nearby houses. The only example of this type of street still existing in London is Lovat Lane on the south side of Eastcheap. It is a very narrow street with its central gully running down the hill towards the Thames. In spite of the slope it would have needed a very heavy rain storm to make sure that all the rubbish was carried into the river.

The Great Buildings of Tudor London

When Henry VII came to the throne the country was Roman Catholic, but by the time Elizabeth died England was officially Anglican. Throughout the reign of Henry VII about one third of England, and nearly half of the land of the City, belonged to the Church, but by the time Elizabeth died nearly all this land had been taken by the Crown and redistributed with very little benefit to the ordinary citizen. Henry's accession can be said to mark the end of the Middle Ages. The ritualistic church services were being criticised, many of the church's superstitions —the power of relics especially—were losing their hold on people's minds, the Bible was soon to be translated into English. Many of the Monasteries and Friaries with their armies of clerks and hangers on were being denounced and exposed, and there was an awakening interest in the world beyond Europe and a growth of new ideas on things like astronomy, mathematics, and navigation. Henry VII did away with the nobles' 'Liveries' (private armies), thereby reducing the risks of internal squabbles. The abolition of liveried retainers also did away with the need for the great town houses of the aristocracy. For example, at his house in Warwick Square, off Newark Lane, Newgate Street, the Earl of Warwick used to keep a private army of up to 600 men at a time. 'Livery' in those days meant a great deal more than it does today, for the noblemen to whom allegiance was given not only provided the uniform but board and lodging, pay, and a share in the plunder of conquest. The more powerful the nobleman, the more deference paid to those wearing his livery.

Cardinal Morton, Henry VII's chief tax inspector, has left us a very fine red-brick gate tower to Lambeth Palace, the London residence of the Archbishops of Canterbury for 750 years. The tower was built in 1490 with an Audience Chamber over the archway and it was here that Thomas More served as page to Morton.

Lambeth Palace can be visited by special arrangement, application should be made to the Chaplain to the Archbishop.

The City Guild Companies were well treated by the King and he confirmed the Hansa Merchants in their privileged trade position. They were called the 'Easterlings' and continued to enjoy their property and privileges until 1551, when, as the result of complaints laid against them, the Liberty of the 'Steel Yard' (the area in which they had settled) was seized into the King's hands and their special privileges revoked. Eventually, in 1598, they were peremptorily ordered to leave the Steel Yard completely and get out of the kingdom. The buildings then came into the possession of the Queen and were used as a Navy Office. The 'Easterlings' had lived in London on the site now covered by Cannon Street Station in Upper Thames Street since the 10th century and their business conduct was so satisfactory and trustworthy that the name Easterling has come down to us corrupted into the word 'Sterling'.

Another notable event of Henry VII's reign was the revival of the Court of the 'Star Chamber'. By influence and oppression it was very often difficult for poor people to get honest verdicts from the courts. The Court of the Star Chamber was made up of one of the Judges and some of the King's officers who were completely unafraid of any nobleman in England, and thus able to give verdicts against the most powerful people in the country. This court later fell into disrepute and was abolished in the 17th century. Its name was derived from the decoration of the ceiling of the chamber at Westminster in which it sat, and there is still a 'Star Chamber Court' in the buildings of the Houses of Parliament at Westminster.

Tudor interior architecture: a finely decorated doorway from the Charterhouse

Greenwich Palace

In 1428 Humphrey, Duke of Gloucester, and brother to Henry V, had obtained, by a somewhat doubtful process of exchange, a parcel of land of some 200 acres at Greenwich on which he had built a home for himself which he called Bella Court. It subsequently came into the hands of his nephew Henry VI and after Duke Humphrey's death, Margaret of Anjou, Henry VI's wife, continued to live there and enlarged the house. She changed the name of the palace to that of 'Placentia' (the pleasant place) and here Henry VIII was born in 1491. It was used throughout Edward IV's reign and he granted a piece of land within the Palace to the Franciscan Order of Observant

Friars, who built a little house and a church which was used as a Chapel Royal. Elizabeth, the daughter of Edward IV, who later became the wife of Henry VII, was born here, and it became one of her favourite residences. Elizabeth's first son Arthur had been born at Winchester in 1486, and also her daughter Margaret in 1489. When, in 1522, Charles V of Spain paid a Royal Visit to Henry VIII, he sailed in splendour up the Thames with 180 ships, 2,000 retainers and 1,000 horse. Here Henry entertained him with jousts, tournaments and extravagant feasts.

Despite the importance of 'Placentia' at the time, little is left today of the Tudors' riverside palace, except some old building materials which were used later by Wren when he was building the Royal Observatory on the site of the 'Good' Duke Humphrey's house. It had been built between a road and the river bank at Greenwich and, like the Palace of Whitehall, it had to be constructed so that part of the building could form a bridge over the road into the park.

The palace where Henry VIII was born, and which he grew to like so much, lasted many years before Christopher Wren tipped its ruins into the river to make room for his new buildings. All that now remains of 'Placentia' is the crypt of the present 'Queen Anne' building. The Tudor buildings consisted of a range on the river front with a five storey gate set near the centre, the Chapel of the Observant Friars on the west, and a tall range of buildings set back from the river. Between the building and the wall alongside the road was a formal garden with a tilt yard on the east side. A small gate house, which is reputed to be the spot where Raleigh laid down his cloak for Queen Elizabeth, then spanned the Woolwich Road, but this has since become a colonnaded terrace and the newer Romney Road has been made nearer to the river.

Henry VIII carried out a lot of building at Greenwich and employed Holbein on the temporary Great Hall he

21

erected in the Tilt Yard. The King established dockyards further up the river at Deptford and also down river at Chatham. He also set up the workshops at Greenwich that turned out the finest armour ever made in this country. Much of it is now in the collections at the Tower of London and Windsor Castle.

Mary and Elizabeth were both born at Greenwich and, together with Edward, spent much time there as children. The keyboard of an organ in the Parish Church of St. Alphage is believed to be the one on which Elizabeth, Mary, and Thomas Tallis used to play.

Mary and Elizabeth did not use Greenwich often during their reigns, but it was at Deptford that Elizabeth knighted Drake, and later at Greenwich she signed the death warrant of Mary Queen of Scots.

Eltham Palace

Henry VII carried out a certain amount of repair work at Greenwich but he also spent a lot of time at Eltham Palace where Edward IV had just rebuilt the Great Hall and the Moat Bridge. At Eltham Henry built a range of domestic buildings at the side of the Great Hall and it is believed that it was here that Sir Thomas More brought Erasmus to meet the King's children in 1499, although the painting in the Houses of Parliament seems to suggest that it was at Greenwich. Sir Thomas More has other connections with Eltham because his daughter, married to Thomas Roper, lived nearby. The barn of their house is still standing, a Tudor timbered building now used as an Art Gallery and maintained by the Woolwich Corporation.

At Eltham part of the moat still exists and is crossed by Edward IV's bridge. The Hall has been restored by the kindness of Messrs. Courtaulds and some Tudor timber buildings, including the Lord Chancellor's lodging in which Wolsey used to stay, can be seen on Thursdays and Sundays. The buildings are at present occupied by the Royal Army Educational Corps.

Richmond Palace

In addition to his work at Eltham Henry VII also rebuilt the Palace of Shene which had fallen into some disrepair since the death of Richard II's queen. The Palace was seriously damaged by fire in 1499 and between that year and 1501 it was rebuilt: 'girded and encompassed with a strong and mighty brick wall, vained and bent with towers in his each corner and angle and also in his mid-way.'

Henry then renamed the place after his old Earldom of Richmond. Undoubtedly this was a most attractive setting for a Palace, for it was conveniently built on the river bank for easy transport and main sewage disposal. Because this Palace was planned as a whole it was a compact range of buildings. The main gates were set in a curtain wall facing what is now Richmond Green, and this gate still stands.

The gate leads to one courtyard and then a second which was dominated by the Great Hall and Chapel on two of its sides, with a third side closed by the towered and pinnacled Royal Apartments which were said to be 'splendidly magnificent'. A low rectangular gallery stood at the rear facing the river and all the buildings were surrounded by orchards, with an aviary, gardens, fountains, and domestic buildings—these included larders, buttery, poultry houses, kitchens, cistern house, and, set at a distance, 'a large house of office'.

The water supply was not taken from the river but piped in from outside springs. The buildings were constructed of stone, brick and timber with a strong perpendicular Gothic influence, and the whole palace covered 10 acres.

It was here in 1502 that Henry VII's daughter Margaret was formally pledged to King James IV of Scotland and here in April of the same year his son Arthur died at the age of 16. Henry himself died at Richmond and a great procession brought him to Westminster Abbey. Over the coffin was a crowned effigy of the King in his robes. The wooden head from this effigy, possibly by Torrigiani, has been identified by the Keeper of the Muniments at Westminster Abbey and can be seen among the wax effigies which are displayed in the Abbey undercroft.

The Palace was very popular with the early Tudors. Catherine of Aragon had stayed there: Henry himself had waited there impatiently for the sound of the cannon that told him Anne Boleyn's head was off; it became a home for Ann of Cleves; and Mary Tudor brought her husband Philip to live there after their marriage. It also became a favourite home for Elizabeth.

A wing called Wardrobe Court still remains, although it was altered in Queen Anne's time. There is the brass memorial of Robert Cotton, the Wardrobe Keeper of Mary Tudor and Elizabeth, in Richmond Church. He no doubt had his problems dealing with Elizabeth's wardrobe which was supposed to have included nearly 2,000 dresses.

In the reign of Elizabeth, Henry and Philip Sydney, father and son, stayed at Richmond Palace. Sir Henry was Keeper of the Queen's Ordnance, and because he found, as Samuel Pepys and others found after him, that even pieces of the Queen's Ordnance got stolen, he ordered all pieces should be marked with his own personal heraldic 'Pheon'—an Arrow Head. Hence the 'Broad Arrow' mark for Government property today.

Sir Walter Raleigh brought Edmund Spenser to read his 'Fairie Queene' to Elizabeth and she thought it to be 'of wondrous worth'—£100 worth she said, but Spenser had to write:

> 'I was promised on a tyme
> To have a reason for my rhyme
> Since that time until this season
> I have had nor rhyme nor reason'

before he got the money.

A symbol of the Renaissance and the growing interest in science and exploration, an astrolabe, an instrument used in astronomy

Westminster Abbey

One evening, before he was captured by Edward IV and murdered in the Tower of London, Henry VI went to Westminster Abbey to pick the spot where he would be buried, but did not decide on the first visit. Later he went back and made up his mind, and a mason marked out the space with a chisel. He had chosen a spot on the north side of the tomb of Edward the Confessor, but the area is now covered with linoleum so that the marks cannot be seen. The tomb was ordered but nothing further was done. When Henry died in the Tower, his body was taken to Chertsey, where it was said miracles began happening near the tomb. Later, Richard III had the body moved to St. George's Chapel at Windsor, where the tomb was placed near the Chapel's relics, at the opposite end of the altar to the tomb of Edward IV, the man who was probably responsible for Henry's murder.

Public feelings now began to have their effect, effigies of Henry VI were set up in various places and people

25

began to make pilgrimages to them. It was felt that Henry VI would be canonised as a saint. Henry VII could not ignore this situation, and he said he would reconstruct the Chapel at Windsor, to receive the remains of the dead king. But Chertsey and Westminster put in a claim for the remains of the prospective saint. Chertsey said Richard III had taken the body by force, Westminster claimed it because Westminster was the place Henry VI had chosen. A council was assembled at Greenwich to consider the matter and decided in favour of Westminster. The Chapter at Windsor resisted this decision on the grounds that it already had the body. However, Westminster began to prepare to receive the body and in his usual practice, Henry VII complained about the expense he was being put to, insisting that the Abbey paid for the transference of the 'Holy Body'.

The King decided to build a more magnificent Chapel at Westminster than he had originally proposed at Windsor, and the Pope granted a licence for the change but the canonization he had promised was not forthcoming so that Henry VI never did become a saint.

The Chapel therefore became the Chapel of Henry VII and it certainly was most magnificent, both inside and out. It was founded as a Chantry with its own Monks, and Torrigiano, a contemporary of Michaelangelo, worked on the effigies. The Chapel suffered badly from Puritan fervour especially in one remarkable way; they destroyed all the saintly figures on the outside but left pedestals with each name intact, and erased all the names on the inside but left the figures!

The Chapel must be seen to be appreciated. Many other monarchs up to George II are buried there but just go and look at the roof vaulting and remember that it was started in 1503 just six years before Henry VII died. You may also notice one empty niche in the north wall of the 'Battle of Britain' Chapel; it appears to have been intended for a statue of Henry VII, but Henry VIII was too preoccupied to have the figure installed. There is a fine bust of Henry VII by Torrigiano in the Victoria and Albert Museum.

The main Nave of the Abbey church was finished under Abbot Islip, whose Chantry is in the north ambulatory, between 1500 and 1532, but the western towers were not built for another 200 years. After the Dissolution a Bishop of Westminster was appointed for the first time, but he resigned in 1550 when the Communion Service was re-introduced. The Mass was back again in 1553.

In 1560 the Monastery was suppressed a second time and a collegiate church founded as a 'Royal Peculiar' with a Dean. Queen Elizabeth refounded the Abbey's School.

Until 1547 the House of Commons continued to sit in the Chapter House but, under Edward VI, St. Stephen's Chapel in the Palace of Westminster was given them for their deliberations. The Crypt of the original Chapel still exists under what is now St. Stephen's corridor.

When Henry VII died in 1509 he left behind a form of royal despotism which his son was to exploit to the full. He also left a foundation for Mercantile greatness to come; he had given a Charter to the Merchant Adventurers, he left a Dockyard at Portsmouth, some beautiful buildings such as Magdalen Tower, Oxford, and 'King Harry Tower', Canterbury, and completed Eton College Chapel, and St. George's Chapel, Windsor—as well as a lot of money for his son to squander. Also, he had left the finest example of Perpendicular Gothic church building in existence in London—the Abbey where he is buried at Westminster together with his Queen, Elizabeth of York.

The Abbey has an extra unexpected attraction in its waxwork collection. Originally it was customary for the bodies of important persons to be carried during their funerals in such a manner that everyone could see and recognise the person being buried. This was so that those present could vouch for the honesty of the proceedings.

Later a carved effigy was carried and, when the art was perfected, a wax effigy was used.

After the burial the effigy was left behind and the collection at the Abbey arose in this manner.

You can see a fine carved head of Henry VII, his Queen, Elizabeth of York, and a wax effigy of Queen Elizabeth which does not have its original head. They are in the undercroft.

The area where the Sanctuary actually stood is marked by the names Great and Little Sanctuary. It was abolished in 1642.

The principal building stood near the west gate of the Abbey precinct, the Gate stood approximately across the end of Tothill Street. It was only removed in the 18th century.

The area around became a refuge for the poor, mainly debtors, who lived in a warren of cheap tenement houses. They were not all just poor unfortunates. Many used the place as a retreat between expeditions of pocket picking and thieving. One street became known as Thieving Lane in Georgian times.

This was the Sanctuary to which Elizabeth Woodville (Henry VII's mother-in-law) fled with her son the Duke of York, after Richard III had taken her other son Edward, the rightful heir, to the Tower.

Henry VIII and Wolsey

In addition to leaving a substantial treasure, Henry VII left the organisation to collect more. The Civil Service was run on the cheap by the simple expedient of using the Church officials to carry out the State administration. The Church paid for them and the people paid for the Church. Although less of the tithe collected by the Church now went to Rome the collection of 'Peter's Pence' was resented by many. When he came to the throne Henry VIII was 18 years old, full of vitality, good at hawking, hunting, wrestling, and dancing. He was 6 foot 2 inches tall, with thinning auburn hair. He was scholarly, a skilled musician, a poet, and a supreme egotist. He married Catherine of Aragon at Greenwich on the 11th June 1509, one week after his Coronation, and she produced a still-born daughter in 1510. From this time until 1518, she produced several children all of which were stillborn or died soon afterwards except Mary in 1516. She was the only child that survived and Queen Catherine had only one more miscarriage in 1518. Elizabeth Blount produced Henry's one illegitimate son in 1519. With the possible exception of Mary Boleyn, Ann's sister, she was the only known mistress in his life. Her son was christened Henry Fitzroy and lived as the Duke of Richmond until July 1536 which was a few months after Ann Boleyn had been executed.

Within six months of Henry's Coronation, Wolsey appears on the scene, and the combination of these two —Minister and Monarch—began. Wolsey was born in 1475, the son of a butcher of Ipswich. He became Bursar of New College, Oxford, a Bachelor of Arts at 15 years of age, Fellow and Schoolmaster at Magdalen College, Oxford, and Chaplain to a Bishop at the Court of Henry VII. In November 1509, Henry VIII made him King's Almoner and Privy Councillor. He was 18 years older than the King and in 1511, although he was ordained to the church and sworn to celibacy, he had married and had fathered a son and daughter. He had a long political career and did not fall out of favour with Henry until 1529. He died in 1530. It has been said of his career, that 'It was one long pageant interspersed with scenes of special and dramatic brilliancy'. It has also been said that 'he rode the papacy to death in this country'. Throughout his life he was guilty of pluralism (the practice of holding more than one office) to the greatest degree. During the greatest period of his ascendency he held, without ever needing to perform the actual duties involved, except that of Lord Chancellor, the positions of: Dean of Tournai, Bishop of Lincoln, Archbishop of York, Abbot of St. Albans, Bishop of Bath and Wells, Bishop of Winchester, Cardinal, and Papal Legate.

The Great Seal of Henry VIII: the king sits in majesty holding the symbols of his power

He was, on three occasions, a candidate for the Papacy, but he was not able to influence the Cardinals sufficiently for them to elect him. As Papal Legate he controlled all church appointments and the right to visit and inspect all religious establishments in England. He extracted fees for appointments at the rate of about 4 per cent per annum from every benefice he visited. He took regular fees for the probate of wills, not only for York but also for Canterbury, although he was never Archbishop of Canterbury. During this time he had power great enough to reform both the monastic and secular clergy but he did not use it. He never visited any of his bishoprics, except for spending a few days at York just before he died.

Wolsey also made sure that his son was well looked after. His son—Thomas Winter—took minor orders at the age of 10 and was given a parish. At 13 he was Dean of Wells, at 14 Provost of St. Peters, Beverley, Archdeacon of York and Richmond, and Chancellor of Salisbury. At 15 he had five prebends at various cathedrals and two rectories. His father later made grants and suggestions that he should be the Bishop of Durham.

Throughout his life Wolsey carried out his duties for Henry with the utmost efficiency, always working for a balance of power on the Continent which would ensure peace. There is no evidence of his being a religious man; to him the Church was a source of income and power, and as a consequence he was not a religious persecutor. There is no record of any execution of heretics in his time; these were to come after his death.

Whitehall Palace

As Archbishop of York, Wolsey took over the London house of the Archbishops known as York Place, which stood on the river bank just north of the Palace of Westminster on the road from Charing Cross to the Palace, and immediately began to enlarge the range of buildings.

He built a great hall on what is now Horse Guards Avenue, immediately opposite the Horse Guards, he planted an orchard on the south side, where the Board of Trade building now stands, and he obtained possession of a number of tenements on the north side. He bought the area known as Scotland Yard and constructed a Chapel which afterwards became the Chapel Royal. There are no illustrations of this palace but it is known that he entertained lavishly in it, inviting numerous foreign dignitaries, in addition, of course, to Henry VIII and many of his Court. In 1957, when the Board of Trade building was being constructed, the wine cellar of the great hall was found below road level. It was lifted intact, put back on a new foundation under the Board of Trade building and can now be visited by arrangement with the Ministry of Works. It is a vaulted chamber 56 feet in length and provides stopes for the barrels of wine which it originally contained.

Anne Boleyn's gateway at Hampton Court

When he was in London at this time Henry only had Greenwich, Eltham, Bridewell, Richmond, the Tower of London, Baynards Castle, Windsor Castle, and a very dilapidated Palace of Westminster to live in. The Palace of Westminster had been largely burned down in 1512 and a small Palace at Bridewell had been started in 1515 under Wolsey. When Wolsey was deposed in 1529 Henry could not wait to move up the river to take over this new modern residence. He conveniently forgot that it belonged to the See of York and that it had not been Wolsey's personal property—besides, he needed a more sumptuous residence for his new Queen.

York Place was said to have consisted of 'one mesuage, two gardens and three acres of land'. The Palace was renamed 'Whitehall' and Henry immediately started to enlarge it. A right of way called King Street, running from Charing Cross to St. Margaret's Church, went past the Palace, and from that street a lane led to some stairs on the river—even Henry was not prepared to close these, so he had to build over and around them.

He 'acquired' from Abbot Islip of Westminster a parcel of land with 'all mesuages, houses, barns, stables, dove houses, orchards, gardens, ponds, fisheries, waters, ditches, lands, meadows and pastures and all and singular their appertanences in any manner belonging to this said great mesuage or tenement'.

This amounted to all that which is now covered by St. James's Park, Green Park, Buckingham Palace and its grounds, Whitehall from Charing Cross to Downing Street, about 23 or 24 acres in all. For a comparison in size, one should consider Hampton Court which covers about 7 or 8 acres; St. James's Palace about 4 acres; and Buckingham Palace about 2 acres.

In addition to this Henry gave himself hunting rights over the land north and west of the Palace. The order said:

For as much as the King's most Royal Majesty is most

desirous to have the games of hare, partridge, pheasant, and heron preserved in and about his honour at his Palace of Westminster, for his own disport and pastime to St. Giles in the Fields, to Our Lady of the Oak, to Highgate, to Hornsey Park, to Hampstead Heath; and from thence to his said Palace of Westminster to be preserved and kept for his own disport, pleasure and recreation. His Highness therefore straightly charges and commandeth all and singular his subjects of what estate degree or condition so ever they be that they nor any of them do presume or attempt to hunt or to hawk or in any means to take or kill any of the said games, within the precincts aforesaid as they tender his favour and will eschew the imprisonment of their bodies and further punishment at His Majesties will and pleasure.

Henry built two great gateways over King Street to enable him to get from his Palace on the riverside to the land on the other side of the street. He also built Whitehall Gate to enable him to get from the south side of his palace to the north side and this stretched over the right of way that led down to the riverside stairs. Whitehall Gate was at the Whitehall (Street) end of what is now Horse Guards Avenue; King's Gate and Holbein Gate were across part of the street that we now know as Whitehall; King's Gate was slightly north of the end of Downing Street and Holbein Gate just at the south end of the banqueting house which stands almost opposite the Horse Guards. On the west side of Whitehall Henry built a cockpit, tennis court and tilt yard. The tilt yard occupied the site of what is now Horse Guards Parade and the Great Close stood on the site of the present Treasury.

Whitehall Palace was almost completely destroyed by fire in 1698 after various schemes for rebuilding had been considered, started, and stopped. The best building left to us is the Banqueting Hall in Whitehall built by Inigo Jones between 1619 and 1622; it was the only part which

34

was completed of a comprehensive plan for the total rebuilding of the palace after an earlier fire in 1619.

One other small relic of the buildings which were destroyed in 1698 remains and is known as 'Queen Mary's Stairs'. These were part of the special riverside stairs built for Queen Mary II to use when she went by boat on the Thames. Because of the later construction of the Embankment they now only lead down to a patch of grass. They are at the Embankment end of Horse Guards Avenue along the Thames frontage of the Board of Trade Building.

All this was only the beginning; Henry next acquired another large parcel of land from Eton College; this was in exchange for some land in Kent and Suffolk. He dissolved a nuns' leper house called St. James's Hospital, and started building St. James's Palace on the site. He engaged the very best craftsmen in the country. The vicar of Kingston supplied the bricks, Caen stone came from Normandy, and 300 ounces of fine gold were needed to gild the initials of Henry and Anne. Holbein did not design the Holbein Gate in which he may have lived, but he may have designed St. James's Palace. Thomas Cromwell, Henry VIII's chancellor, directed the two hundred and eleven workmen and six clerks for 18 months. Bowling alleys, tennis courts, draining and fencing of what is now St. James's Park were all completed, but the palace was not furnished with water closets! It was nearly 200 years before they arrived. Only the Gate Tower, the Presence Chamber, the Chapel Royal and Guard Room remain, and some of the entwined Hs and As can still be seen.

Anne was married in May 1533 and, after her Coronation, spent much time at St. James's often gambling with Henry and winning at dice and cards, partaking of great feasts, and scheming for the benefit of her relations. Henry was disappointed when Anne gave birth to a daughter, but Anne celebrated the death of his previous

35

wife by appearing dressed in yellow against Henry's orders.

It may have been Henry's conduct with Jane Seymour that caused Anne to have a miscarriage later, but it also may have been the fact that Anne saw Henry fall with his horse in full armour. The fall was so heavy that those near him thought he was dead. However, it only left him with an ulcerous sore on his leg which never healed and which eventually put an end to his active life. In time he started becoming fat. Soon after the miscarriage, during a joust at Greenwich, he suddenly got up and left Anne. This was, for Anne, the beginning of the end.

An intricately carved Tudor fireplace, typical of the lavish decoration in the houses of the rich

Hampton Court

In 1514, after he had abandoned the idea of building at Bridewell, Wolsey leased the monastic buildings at Hampton for £50 a year. With this went the right to take four loads of timber yearly from St. John's Wood in Middlesex.

Here Wolsey was to build a real palace, not a fortress. The time had now come when defence was no longer a major consideration for architects; nevertheless a moat was dug but only a token piece of it remains today.

Built of red brick with a great Gate House (originally two storeys higher than it is today), the palace was laid out in spacious courts, the first of which, Base Court, was almost entirely surrounded by guest rooms. It was a quadrangle 160 feet by 140 feet in size, with the guest rooms looking outwards and connected by corridors.

It is possible that from the beginning Wolsey and Henry had an understanding that the building was really the King's Palace; certainly there is little doubt that Henry enjoyed being entertained at Hampton Court. One major difference between the Royal Palaces and Wolsey's show-place was in their floor coverings. In all Henry's palaces most of the rooms still had their earth floors covered with rushes interspersed with the rosemary and herbs that gave off a sweet smell when crushed under foot. As the effect of the herbs wore off, a fresh mixture was thrown on top, and into this mass fell all the household scraps and the droppings of the scavaging animals, until one literally walked on a compost heap. Later Henry issued orders against the admission of dogs but this alone could not have improved the general atmosphere very much.

When the Court was moved elsewhere the whole mass was dug out and replaced with fresh reeds to start all over again. This process was known as 'the sweetening'. The period between 'sweetenings' was controlled by Government order so that the compost could be removed under controlled conditions and broken down for its saltpetre content, which was extracted to make gunpowder. Removal for the 'sweetening' was one of the principal reasons why Queen Elizabeth 'progressed' throughout the country so often. She had a very sensitive nose and complained at her coronation because the anointing oil stank. There was probably one other reason which she may have inherited from her mean grandfather. A visit to a rich courtier for several days cut the cost of living considerably—quite apart from the rich presents she generally received at the end of the visit.

The conditions at Hampton Court were very different for practically all the visitors' rooms were provided with Damascene carpets.

Wolsey had chosen this spot on the Thames because it was healthy and he was rather delicate. Since he was quite determined to see that the chances of disease arising in his country palace would be reduced to the minimum, he provided the hitherto unknown benefits of bathrooms, a very comprehensive drainage system and a specially arranged water supply piped in lead from the other side of the Thames. The drainage at Hampton Court was so good that it was always the healthiest royal palace. It is worth remembering in this connection that as late as the middle of the last century the Prince Consort died of typhoid, probably caught through the bad drains at Windsor.

The whole palace was conceived on a vast scale, built to house up to 600 guests at any one time, as well as Wolsey's own household which included a High Chamberlain, a Vice Chamberlain, and 500 liveried attendants. There were three courts in all covering much the same area as covered today.

Since Wolsey's time there have been considerable alterations in the Clock and Fountain Courts. A description has come down to us of the style enjoyed by the French Embassy which was entertained at Hampton Court by Wolsey in 1527. When the guests arrived they were first shown to their rooms, which were furnished *'with great trussed bedsteads of alabaster with My Lord's Arms and flowers of gilt upon the sides, black velvet high back chairs embossed with a Cardinal's hat, cushions upholstered with cloth of gold, damask tablecloths, a flagon of wine and silver drinking goblets for their refreshment before going to the meal'*.

One example of the growing concern for personal comfort: a fine bedstead with walnut inlay

When all was ready:

A fanfare of trumpets announced the banquet and officers of the household went round the rooms to conduct the guests to their appointed places.

The food appeared in most elaborate shapes, Castles, Houses, a model of Old St. Paul's, Animals, Birds and human forms most likely made and counterfeit in dishes.

and of course Wolsey never neglected the necessity for wine to cheer the occasion. Meals were served on gold plate. Wolsey suffered from dyspepsia and ate sparingly. He never arrived until all his guests were in the hall and seated; very often he did not come until the second course and then made a grand entrance.

39

When guests went back to their rooms they found light refreshment had been provided in every chamber :
Each had a basin and a ewer of silver, some gilt, some parcel gilt a pot with wine or beer and a fine manchet and chetloaf of bread.

One Ambassador reported that he had to pass through eight rooms, each one hung with very fine tapestries which were changed every day, before he reached the Audience Chamber.

Henry first visited Hampton Court with Catherine in 1516 but Wolsey did not consider the palace properly finished until after the Field of the Cloth of Gold in 1520.

Many people believe that buildings continue to carry and induce in others impressions of the people who have lived in them, and that it is the extra sensitive person who can 'feel a presence' or see a ghost. Here at Hampton Court is the place to find Wolsey. If one stands in Base Court one can almost see one of the Cardinal's processions going by.

First came liveried servants in gold and 'byse' (a bright light blue) and then two priests bearing silver crosses, more servants, grooms, and yeomen, then two secular clerks holding aloft great silver pillars as if they were maces, more grooms, gentlemen, and clergy followed by two grooms carrying great poleaxes, more gentlemen and lords, clergy, and knaves; then, borne on a great cushion, the Cardinal's hat, brilliant scarlet, flat crowned, with a wide brim and sixteen great tassels hanging on either side. This was surrounded by an escort of gentlemen, lords, clergy, and knaves; then Wolsey, borne on a great cushion, medium height, pale faced with a body inclined to fatness, but an imposing presence, dressed in a full length red velvet gown, a small round red hat and, round his neck, a crucifix suspended from a thin gold chain. His hands clasped together across his chest he would clutch a cut orange stuffed with sweet herbs and spices into which he continually inserted the rather prominent pontifical nose to ward off stinks and odours. He hoped that this would prevent him catching any illness, especially the sweating sickness or plague. He looked from side to side as he passed and although he did not appear to recognise what he saw, he missed nothing.

At the end of the procession came more servants, grooms, and scullions numbering about one hundred and twenty men and all dressed in Wolsey's gold and blue livery.

But in 1529 it was all over for Wolsey. Henry was in a hurry to move in, but the great palace was not nearly large enough for him, and he therefore started to make it even larger by building the Great Hall. The building accounts tell us that the work went on by night as well as day: 'Empcion of tallow candells spent by the workmen in the nyghte tymes uppon the paving of the hall, for the hasty expedicion of the same at 18d the dosyn.'

And for workmen: 'Workyng in theyre owne tyme and dryngkyng tymes for the haste expedycyon of the same.'

and: 'Payde to John Hethe, paynter ... for gyldying and payntyng 272 badges of Kyngs and Quenys, standing aboughte the bowghte, and the caters within the Kynges new haul at 12d the price.'

and: 'for lyke gyldying and payntyng of 28 hedd, standying uppon the hammer beamys in the rouff of the said haull, price the pece 2s–56s.'

The Hall still stands there today with a fine wine cellar beneath it, very similar to but larger than the one at Whitehall. Henry's workmen built the Great Kitchen that still remains, and between those huge open fires, even on a cold day, it is not difficult to work up a real sweat, if you imagine yourself as a scullion or turnspit of the time when meals were being prepared for five hundred or more guests. Retainers and servants doubled the numbers, many of them sleeping six to a room or in tents when the company was large. These retainers and servants were often lazy, gossiping, and dirty but their shiftlessness does not seem to have prompted the following: 'All such as have their lodgings within the court shall give straight charge to the Ministers and Keepers of their chambers, that they do not cast, leave, or lay any manner of dishes, platters, saucers, or broken meate, either in the said galleries, or at their chambre doores or in the court or other place . . . soe that broken meate and drinke be in no wise lost, cast away or eaten with dogges, nor lye abroad in the galleries and courtes, but may daily be saved for the relief of the poore folks.'

A great chapel, a tilt yard with corner towers, bowling alleys, and a royal tennis court were built. The tennis court with some alterations in Charles II's time remains in full use today for 'Royal' tennis—the oldest place in the world where a ball game has been continuously played. Surrounding all these buildings were gardens, orchards, hedges, arbours, and of course the river which provided easy access to London and most of Henry's other palaces.

'Honeymoon Court' might have been an appropriate name for this place under Henry VIII. All six of his wives came here in turn, two in 1540. Some of the en- twined Hs and As remain from the first frenzied building and there was much hasty tearing down and alteration to change Anne to Jane. Anne of Cleves saw more of the place as a visitor than as a wife, and Catherine Howard's ghost still haunts the Long Gallery. Catherine Parr was married to Henry at Hampton Court in July 1543 and she nursed him there until his death in 1547.

Elizabeth was very fond of the Palace and lived there often, she added one building on the south side overlook- ing her 'Knot Garden'.

The Elizabethan 'Knot Garden' was planned like a

posy laid out on the ground and it was intended to fulfill the same purpose. Geometrical patterns edged with lavender, thrift, or rosemary crammed with sweet smelling flowers or herbs. Sometimes, when flowers were out of season, or to save time and labour, the edges would be of box and the spaces between filled with coloured earths and sands. These of course were not fragrant and Francis Bacon, who was no mean gardener, thought them 'but toys, you may see as good sights many times in tarts'.

The herbs also supplied another need, they could be used to camouflage the semi-putrid taste of the meat. There was no chilled storage, and in winter it could only be kept by salting. This was a real problem for the less wealthy, for the rich and powerful could always arrange a hunt or even knock off a swan or two in winter. It is of interest that Francis Bacon died from the results of catching cold after experimenting with a dead chicken by stuffing it with snow to preserve it!

Charles II replanned the gardens and substantial rebuilding took place at the east end under Christopher Wren in William and Mary's time. We are lucky to have such a large part of the Wolsey and Henry palace left to us, because Wren wanted to pull the whole lot down and start afresh.

There is one final word on Wolsey at Hampton Court which shows, despite his splendour and pomp, how superstitious he really was. For some reason he always avoided any contact with the village of Kingston. When coming from London by road it was on the direct route to Hampton Court but for some reason he always made a detour round it. When in 1530 he had retired to his See at York, this being his first visit, he decided to make one more effort to regain Henry's favour and started on the journey to London. On the way at Leicester, he was intercepted by the Constable of the Tower of London who had been sent by Henry to arrest him. It was only after

Wolsey learned that the Constable's name was Kingston that he became ill and died at Leicester without ever again coming to London.

Royal Nonsuch

In 1509 the Canons of Merton Priory had reported to the Bishop of Winchester that the prior had been keeping women and stealing jewels and they did not want to be victimised for telling tales! The moral quality of the prior, Thomas Mundy, wasn't any better in 1538. By the trick of ante-dating documents and bribing the monks of the Chapter, he portioned out most of the priory's property among his relations just before Thomas Cromwell, King Henry's Vicar General, dissolved the priory on the 13th April 1538.

One week later the King's workmen moved in to the very small village of Cuddington with the first cartloads of stone quarried from the priory buildings. The village was obliterated to make way for the 'King's new workes', and more than 500 workmen laboured to build the Palace of Nonsuch (no other such house). There was certainly no other such house for elegant ostentation, and during the 150 years it stood, its name became synonymous with splendour and magnificence. It was admired throughout Europe. There was a great tower at each end of the over-decorated front, one tower supporting the large cistern from which water was piped all over the building; and a splendid gate house in the centre of the inner court-yard, but there were no bathrooms and no carpets! There were also battlements, parapets, turrets, towers, copulas, chimneys, jackstaves, and painted panels in profusion. There were fountains, ponds, and statues in the extensive gardens. All have now gone except the park.

Elizabeth often visited Nonsuch during her lifetime. Charles II eventually gave it to his mistress Barbara Villiers, who became in turn Lady Castlemain, Countess of Southampton, and Duchess of Cleveland. She sold it for the value of the building materials and it disappeared so completely that even the site is not accurately known. The whole palace became a half-remembered myth.

Excavations started in 1958 have disclosed much information about the extent of this further example of Henry's arrogance, extravagance, and love of display. One can understand why Henry had to devalue the currency before he died.

One of the most remarkable events at Nonsuch took place in 1559 when Elizabeth, aged 25, included Nonsuch in her summer progress, going there from Eltham. The Lord High Steward, the Earl of Arundel who was a man of 40 and twice widowed, aspired to the hand of Elizabeth, and he entertained her grandly at Nonsuch.

The event was the most costly and elaborate ever seen there; with banquets, feasts, masques, plays, musicians, and a handsome gift of a 'cupboard' of gold plate to cap the display. Elizabeth, however, was not the marrying kind and Arundel was kept dangling.

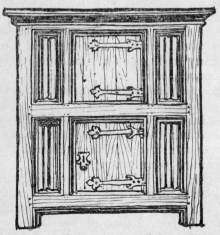

An oak cupboard used for storing all household possessions

The Dissolution of the Monasteries

Between 1525 and 1536 Henry bullied Parliament and the Church into accepting him as 'Supreme Head of the English Church'. By reviving an old law of Edward III and passing new ones, the Pope's power in this country was finally broken, but Henry did not become a Protestant, his religion was to be the 'Middle way' and he showed this by executing both Protestants and Roman Catholics for their beliefs.

Wolsey had shown that extra revenue could be collected by dissolving small monasteries and convents. By this time Henry had begun to run short of money and Thomas Cromwell, after his appointment as 'Vicar General in matters ecclesiastical', was not only ready, but eager to re-line Henry's pockets.

In 1535 Royal Commissioners were sent throughout the country to look into the condition of the monasteries, and the same year the first victims of Henry's doctrine of 'Royal Supremacy' were executed.

Bishop Fisher and Sir Thomas More were both tried in Westminster Hall, and both found guilty of refusing to take the oath that acknowledged Henry as head of the Church. John Fisher, Bishop of Rochester, was found guilty 'to hang at Tyburn', but the King's so-called clemency changed it to mere beheading at Tower Hill.

Sir Thomas More, Recorder of London, Speaker of the House of Commons, and Lord Chancellor (after the fall of Wolsey) resigned when the bulk of the clergy surrendered to Henry in 1532. He retired to live in his house at Chelsea, which stood between Beaufort Street and King's Road and Milman Street. The house was later rebuilt by Robert Cecil and had a series of famous owners including the Duke of Buckingham, the Duke of Beaufort, and Sir Hans Sloane. The stable yard on the corner of Milman Street and King's Road became a Moravian burial ground and the west wall is believed to be the last remaining relic of More's house. The Sir Thomas More Chapel in Chelsea Old Church survived the last war although the church was badly damaged.

Sir Thomas More was willing to accept Anne and her children for succession to the throne, but would not accept Henry in place of the Pope. He was charged with high treason and chose to remain silent. He was convicted on the lies of a previous protégé, Richard Rich, and executed.

In the twenty-six-year period that followed, all the monastic and other foundations were liquidated. The first casualties were the minor monasteries, then the great monsteries, followed by the friaries and last, to squeeze out the last drop of treasure, the chantries.

Christ Church (Holy Trinity), Aldgate

In London one of the first foundations affected was Holy Trinity (Christ Church), a foundation of Augustinian Canons. An interesting walk around the area today starts at St. Catherine Cree Church in Leadenhall Street (Cree is derived from 'Christ'). It was the church for the parishioners, for they were not allowed to use the very much larger priory church, which was reserved for the monks. The church standing there today was probably built by Inigo Jones between 1628 and 1630. At the east end of the church there was a pathway leading through to the churchyard. The priory wall stretched all along the way on the left on the road towards Aldgate which bears left to the corner of Duke's Place, and behind it were two great gardens surrounding the priory church. This consisted of a nave, chancel, and Lady Chapel. It had been founded by Queen Matilda, the wife of Henry I, in 1108. One then turns into Duke's Place, which was 'a way' between the priory wall on the left and the city wall on the right; the John Cass School was built on the garden. On the left is St. James's Passage which was cut across the priory kitchen and other domestic buildings. Turn into this and just before you enter Mitre Square, on the right, stood the Frator (dining hall) and on the left the Dortor (dormitory). Mitre Square was the churchyard of the Prior. On the left where the plaque says 'St. James's Church' stood the chapter house. St. James's Church was built after the dissolution on the site of the chapter house and honours King James I.

Return to Duke's Place and continue westward, the ruins of the great synagogue on your left stand on the site of more domestic buildings of the priory and the kitchen garden. Turn left into Creechurch Lane and left again into Creechurch Place and you are now standing in the Great Court of the priory. On the right stood the wall facing out to Heneage Lane which was the western boundary of the priory and the way used by the parish people to get to their Church of St. Catherine Cree. Today's Creechurch Lane, once called King Street, was the way to the priory main gate; opposite stood the great church of the priory.

Continue diagonally left across Creechurch Place and turn into the narrow passage. This cuts through the site of the Prior's house, and brings you into Mitre Square. If you then go across the square into Mitre Street and look along to the left (towards Aldgate), you will be looking along the whole length of the priory church. Mitre Street was built right through the length of the church.

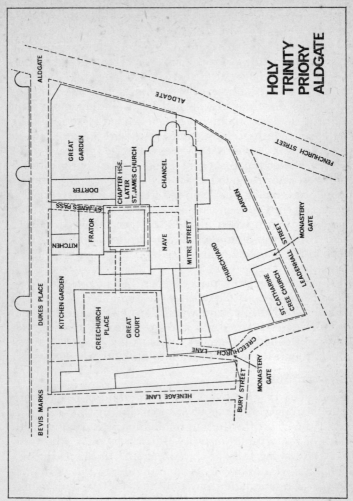

Holy Trinity Priory: the dotted lines show existing streets, and the solid lines indicate the Tudor buildings

The prior was automatically an Alderman of the City but he was eligible to become Lord Mayor. This non-elective presentation of an Alderman continued until the dissolution of the priory. In the year 1439 the Common Council had to appeal to the Lord Mayor and Aldermen to try to prevent a new prior becoming an Alderman because the dissolute life he had been leading made him unsuitable. The Common Council obviously set a higher standard than the church but they were unsuccessful in their appeal. Perhaps they were justified, because just 63 years later the Bishop of London was trying to have the then prior removed because too much of the priory's money was being spent on a certain Mrs. Hodges. The prior and the eighteen canons do not seem to have offered much resistance when in 1532 they were called upon to sign a deed handing over the monastery and all its possessions. It was believed to have been one of the richest in existence.

Henry granted the priory to Sir Thomas Audley who later become Lord Chancellor, his daughter became the Duchess of Norfolk, and when the Duke came to leave there, Duke's Place came into existence. A new church was built called St. James's, perhaps because the parishioners found it too far to walk to St. Catherine's Cree.

Charterhouse

Another early 'take over' was Charterhouse, but there a much stronger resistance was put up by the religious occupants. This Carthusian foundation was a house with rules of remarkable austerity. What was more, the rules were still being fully observed in 1532. In this Order the monks lived solitary lives in individual cells arranged around a quadrangle, they only met their fellow monks in silence, for services—Mass, Matins, and Evensong. They only communicated once a week when they took a walk and a vegetarian meal together. They retired at seven and were aroused at eleven for midnight Matins which was carried out under conditions of utmost rigour. The monks had to sing the Office at the slowest possible pace to test their physical and mental power to the utmost. This service would last until about two o'clock when the monks again retired until 5 am at which time they arose for the day. Sir Thomas More went there to live for four years and afterwards always wore the hair shirt of the monks.

The Carthusian prior in London was John Houghton and he, together with two other priors of the Order, found himself unable to accept Henry VIII as Head of the Church. Houghton was put into the Tower, tried at Westminster, and condemned, he was then hung at Tyburn, cut down, disembowelled whilst still alive, and thereafter quartered. Part of John Houghton was hung on the gatehouse which still exists at the entrance to Charterhouse. Later three Carthusian monks were executed and two were hung in chains at York. Eleven monks were left chained upright in Newgate Gaol until ten had died of filth and disease and only one survived to be executed.

The priory was valued at £642.0.4½ and Henry promptly looted timber, stones, glass, and even trees from the orchard and carp from the pond.

In 1545 what was left of Charterhouse was granted to the Chancellor of the Court of Augmentations, a special court for dealing with the suppression of the monasteries. This was Sir Edward North who entertained Queen Elizabeth at Charterhouse on two occasions. Eventually his son sold it to the Duke of Norfolk who had narrowly escaped execution under Henry VIII.

Thomas Howard, Duke of Norfolk changed the name of Charterhouse to Howard House and started to rebuild and improve the buildings. Most of these improvements disappeared as the result of the last war. However, he could not keep out of trouble, and he went to the Tower of London for attempting to marry Mary Queen of Scots. After being released he again intrigued against Queen

Elizabeth and eventually he was beheaded on Tower Hill in 1572.

His son Phillip inherited his estate, turned Roman Catholic and was imprisoned in the Tower of London, where he died in 1595. He is commemorated by an inscription he carved in Beauchamp Tower.

The house then passed to Elizabeth's 'Good Thomas' Howard who had led the English fleet against the Armada and he entertained Elizabeth once more at Charterhouse. He was created Earl of Suffolk but, because he was building Audley End, one of the finest houses in Essex, he became short of money and therefore sold Charterhouse to Thomas Sutton for £13,000.

Thomas Sutton was a rich coal merchant, who founded 'The Hospital of King James in Charterhouse' in 1611. King James had stayed at the house on his arrival from Scotland and provided himself with some pocket money on the occasion by creating over one hundred Knights at about £1,000 a time. The hospital housed eighty old men and the school forty boys. Both still exist: the hospital where it was founded, and the now famous

A goblet of oriental agate mounted in silver-gilt. It has a London Hallmark for 1567–68

school at Godalming where it was moved in 1872.

Although the place was badly damaged during the war, it has been well restored, and visits can be arranged by application to the Registrar.

Most of the religious houses were disposed of with little or no resistance on the part of the monks, and there were always opportunists waiting for the Royal Favour which would allow them to descend like vultures and tear at the remains. The buildings were made of good stone, timber, and most valuable of all, many had lead roofs, which accounts for the vast amount of de-roofing that took place.

The behaviour of many of the monks was little better, they were bribed into handing over their monasteries peacefully by offers of pensions (surprisingly many of which were paid), benefices and church offices. Several priors became bishops or archdeacons.

In many cases the monasteries were already vacated by monks who had left their orders to adopt secular life. It has been estimated that there were no more than 5,000 monks, 1,600 friars, and 2,000 nuns in the whole country at the time of the Dissolution.

Although the ordinary people felt that some change was necessary, and most of the religious population acquiesced in the Dissolution, Cromwell and his men were well prepared with proof of the corruptness of the Church to prevent any opposition. The well staged public destruction of the 'Boxley Rood of Grace' at St. Paul's Cross on Sunday, 24th February 1538 is an instance.

The Rood was a large, elaborately carved figure of Christ on the Cross which had been acquired by Boxley in legendary manner in the 13th century. The legend said that:

'the rood was carved by an English carpenter who having served as a soldier was held captive on the Continent.' *He intended that when eventually he was freed he would sell the Rood in England. When that time came he ob-*

tained transport to Gravesend, Kent. As soon as he was ashore, he loaded his Rood on to the back of an ass and moved off to Rochester where he stopped to eat, but while doing so the animal with its load bolted out of the town. The owner gave chase and although he was able to receive tidings of the animal's movements from people who had seen it, he did not catch up with it until it had reached Boxley, a small village just north of Maidstone.'

At Boxley stood a Cistercian abbey, the monks of which, for some time, had been watching the pilgrims on their way to Canterbury along a road a few miles from their abbey, but never making the detour that would have brought some fame and fortune to their house.

When the carpenter reached Boxley he found the ass with its load inside the abbey, and despite continuous efforts by all present the ass refused to move until the owner had to agree to unload the Rood. The animal was now led quietly outside to graze, but the Rood, resting against a pillar in the abbey, could not be shifted even by the combined efforts of all present.

The carpenter was finally persuaded that the Rood had arrived at this place by a miracle and must remain. He therefore accepted what recompense the Abbot was prepared to pay and departed.

The arrival of the Rood by divine intervention was soon publicised and people began to visit it. Word spread of the marvellous figure of Christ which scowled or smiled upon those who saw it, according to the value of the gift left for the abbey, and soon many of those heading for Canterbury made the necessary detour.

Boxley Abbey became very rich and prosperous, but in 1538 their Rood provided the most damning evidence of the depths to which some monastic foundations could sink. For when it was exposed and burned at St. Paul's Cross it was shown to be 'Cunningly devised with wood, wire, paste and paper' so that with a monk secreted behind it pulling the correct wires, the facial expression could be changed at will. This was only one of many discoveries which were made in various parts of the country.

The strange thing about Boxley is that the official reason for dissolving the abbey was that there were too many flowers in the garden and therefore the monks had 'used the rents of the Monastery for gilly flowers and roses'!

St. Paul's Cross was chosen for this exposure because it was the place regularly used by the Church for announcing public matters of both church and civic concern. It had been used since Saxon times for such purposes, and until the mid-17th century this was the 'Speaker's Corner' of London and saw the reading of Papal Bulls, announcements of Royal illegitimacies, bible burnings, ranting against Protestants and Popes, penances before executions, and once, a cursing of shoe makers for making pointed toed shoes more than 2 inches long. (It wasn't so much that the church disliked the fashion as the fact that they knew wearers of such shoes would be unwilling to spoil them by kneeling to pray.)

The approximate site in St. Paul's churchyard is marked by an obelisk which was erected in 1910. The closures were widespread and most of the sites have left some relic or name by which we can know them. The Franciscan Minoresses of St. Clare left us St. Clare Street and the Minories. A parish church stood there until 1899 and the building was finally destroyed in 1941.

The Cistercians of St. Mary Graces, on the site of which the Royal Mint now stands, have left us East Smithfield and East Minster Street. It is said the Abbey was sometimes known as 'East Minster' but there is no authority for this.

The College of St. Spirit and St. Mary, Richard Whittington's foundation, has left us College Hill and a wall plaque in 'the Vintry', near Upper Thames Street.

St. John's Clerkenwell

The Priory of St. John of Jerusalem has left us more remains than others. This great foundation had been consecrated by the Patriarch of Jerusalem in 1185, for the Knights Hospitallers. The priory occupied 10 acres and stretched from the gate house which still exists in St. John's Lane, to Clerkenwell Green. Like the Temple it had a Round Church, the site of which is still marked by a ring of stones set out in the roadway. The church was destroyed in 1941 by bombs but a new one, assigned to the Order of St. John of Jerusalem, has been built over the Norman and early English crypt which is still in existence.

The gate house, the only ancient one left to us, which spans a road in London, was built in 1504 and later became the publishing offices of the *Gentleman's Magazine* in 1731, where for a time Samuel Johnson worked.

John Stow tells us that at the Dissolution the priory was valued at £262. 19. 0 per annum and Sir William Weston, the prior, did not resist the dissolution but accepted a pension of £1,000 per year. However, he did not live to enjoy this pension and died on the day he signed the deed on 7th May 1540. The Gate House and Church can be visited by application to the Secretary.

St. Martin-le-Grand

St. Martin-le-Grand had been a Royal foundation of Secular Canons enjoying great privileges. Its Charter had been confirmed by William the Conqueror in 1067 with special Rights of Sanctuary and even the Dissolution did not entirely remove this privilege.

Only the name of the street and a plaque on the wall remain today but for many years the Sanctuary gave shelter for many, and its privileges as a 'Liberty' did not finally end until they were abolished by the Act of Parliament which provided for the building of the Post Office in 1815. One of the fugitives who took advantage of this Sanctuary was Miles Forest, one of the murderers of the princes in the Tower of London.

Sanctuaries existed from the earliest time. They were known before Christianity and certainly in Saxon days, possibly even since Roman times. They fulfilled a need for alleviating the harsh laws and punishments, and as a possible protection from powerful officials, revenge seekers, or feuding factions. More generally they gave refuge to those pursued by the 'hue and cry', which all citizens were compelled to take part in by law.

All early churches gave a limited degree of sanctuary to shelter fugitives who thereby placed themselves under the protection of God relying on the fact that sacrilege would be committed by anyone attempting to remove them from the building. Sacrilege was punishable by law even in Saxon times, and anyone who committed it could be flayed alive and his skin fastened to the door of the church. Offenders often paid sums of money to save themselves from this torture—this was known as 'hide-geld'.

Two Chartered Sanctuaries existed in London in Tudor times, one at St. Martin-le-Grand and the other at Westminster. A third 'Liberty' in Whitefriars was added by James I in 1608 and two other 'Liberties' came into existence south of the river—the 'Clink' and the 'Mint'.

St. Martin-le-Grand Church was pulled down in 1548 and new buildings erected including a prison and court with a bailiff. It remained a refuge for debtors for another century and a half.

St. Helen's Bishopsgate

A good deal more has been left for us to see at St. Helen's, Bishopsgate. As this corner of the City escaped the Great Fire of London in 1666 much early work is left and the remains include part of the Nuns' Church with the parish church built alongside.

Legend has it that the Roman Emperor Constantine

founded the first church here on the site of a pagan temple in the 4th century when he was converted to Christianity.

The dedication is to his mother Helena, the daughter of 'Old King Cole' and the reputed discoverer of the true cross. St. Helen's was one of many churches throughout Europe that venerated pieces of the true cross.

A priory had been founded as a Benedictine nunnery in 1212 under the control of the Dean of St. Paul's and successive deans had to take action to enforce the rules of the convent. From time to time the nuns were told that they must 'abstain from kissing secular persons, a custom to which they had hitherto been too prone'. The prioress was to give up all her little dogs except one or two, the nuns must not alter their dresses to make them more fashionable or 'unduly ostentatious unless necessity so demanded', and they must not hurry through their services in their anxiety to get on with the music and dancing at Easter and Christmas! The priory was dissolved in 1538 and was valued at £314.2.6. The prioress and the nuns were pensioned and the buildings passed into the hands of Sir Richard Williams, Thomas Cromwell's nephew. He sold them to the Leather Sellers' Company, who still own a large part of the site and have their Hall there.

By a ruthless act of vandalism all the buildings, which even the Great Fire had not destroyed, were demolished, but the church, which has been called the 'Westminster Abbey of the City', has been left.

Pay it a visit and look for the tomb of Julius Caesar, one of the great lawyers of the 16th century, who had a sealed legal agreement with God inscribed on his tomb to die when his time came. Even his legal brain, as Master of the Rolls, would have found it difficult to break that agreement!

There you can also see where Sir Thomas Gresham is buried. He built the first Royal Exchange and founded

Gresham College but he never got round to putting the steeple on St. Helen's as he had promised. Very close by you will find the founder of Tonbridge School, another of the 'New' men—Sir Andrew Judd. He was a Skinner and you may note from the Skinners' Arms plates attached to the buildings on the left outside the church that they belonged to that Company. They were donated by Andrew Judd in 1558 with other properties to make certain payments to six alms folk in St. Helen's; 'each 8d a week and £1.5.4 per annum for coal amongst them and the Company's Warden 10s per annum for his trouble in making the distributions'.

Perhaps Francis Bancroft, a Draper, who endowed almshouses and a school at Woodford in Essex, left the most trying task to the Wardens of his Company, when he had his tomb made with a lid so that once a year they could come and open it to see if he was still there! It is to their credit that they kept up this custom for a hundred years before the task became altogether too distasteful.

A jug of Rhenish stoneware mounted in silver-gilt. It has a London hallmark for 1597–98

St. Bartholomew's

All that is left of the priory and hospital of St. Bartholomew's which was dissolved in 1539 is the choir of the original Norman building with later additions.

The nave was destroyed and the choir reserved for the parish. The rest was sold to Sir Richard Rich, Thomas Cromwell's son-in-law and the betrayer of Sir Thomas More. He proceeded to strip it and to let out the remaining buildings.

The treatment of these buildings reflects no credit on any of those concerned. In Queen Elizabeth's time the Bishop of London even stripped the lead off the roof of the church! Factories, coal cellars, printing works, a forge, a public house, and stables were placed within the church buildings and cloister. Only the hard work and devotion of later rectors and generous donors has recovered a piece of one of the earliest buildings left in the City. The timber framed building over the west gate was built in 1595 and this wasn't realised until 1916, when a bomb blew the tiles off the front, and disclosed the Tudor construction beneath.

Just in front of this building was the site for many executions under the Tudors and particularly under Mary, on charges of poisoning, murder, and whatever was the particular heresy of the moment.

Executions did not start on this spot with the Tudors; the first, which is recorded by a plaque on the site, is that of William Wallace in 1305, but there are some indications that he may in fact have been executed at Tyburn.

A much more gentle and humane event now takes place annually within a few yards of this execution spot. On Good Friday, in the churchyard occupying the site of the nave of the old church, the Butterworth Charity is dispensed after church service. The origin of the custom is not known but the first reference is made to it in 1686. The Charity takes the form of providing widows of the parish with a sixpence and a Hot Cross Bun. These are laid on a tombstone in the churchyard where the congregation and clergy are assembled for the ceremony. In recent years the small sum of 6d has been added to from the collection taken from the congregation of the previous year.

For his expenditure of £1,064.11.3 Sir Richard Rich not only obtained all the buildings but he also received all the rights in the annual St. Bartholomew Fair. This had first been granted to Rahere, the founder of the monastery and hospital, by Henry I in 1133.

All other fairs were prohibited whilst this one was in progress. All travellers were to be allowed free movement to and from the fair without interference by the King's Officers—unless the Canons of St. Bartholomew's asked for help. These fairs which were conducted for the purpose of sale and barter gave the holder the right by Charter to extract a toll for every transaction carried out. A court was appointed from the traders present, overseen by an officer of the Prior. Most probably it was held at the original site of the court, known as the 'Pie Powder' court (from 'Pied Poudre' meaning dusty shoes), a tavern which stood in Giltspur Street at the corner of Cock Lane, known as Pie Corner. This Court mainly had jurisdiction over commercial matters but it could also arrest and punish thieves or vagabonds if it was proved they were captured within the bounds of the fair.

By the time Richard Rich came into possession, the fair had degenerated from its original purpose of buying and selling into one long continuous funfair with all the attendant wrestling booths, puppet shows, the exhibition of freaks, the barkers with their patent cures, gingerbread, hobby horses, gambling, and ballad singers, in fact all the fun of the fair of the time. It attracted a vast number of highly undesirable persons, not the least of which were the pick-pockets.

Occasionally it was closed down because of the plague

but generally it continued year after year and was usually opened with the attendance of the Lord Mayor and Court of Aldermen in their robes. In 1614 Ben Jonson produced his play called *Bartholomew Fair* and many other plays have mentioned it, giving some idea of the atmosphere of the junketings. The fair continued growing in proportions until it lasted for fourteen days and then was again restricted to three days, in line with the original grant. Complaints about the nuisance increased and eventually in the 1830s the City Companies bought the old priory rights from the descendants of Lord Rich.

This hospital is second oldest in the country (St. Bartholomew's in Rochester is older) and was surrendered to Henry with the priory in 1539. The loss to the poor people was so serious that the pleas of the City Corporation and in particular the endeavours of Sir Richard Gresham caused Henry to take heed and he finally agreed to its re-foundation in 1544, but he did not actually sign the documents until the year of his death in 1547. He also agreed to endow the hospital with 500 marks per year, provided the City Corporation contributed a similar amount making 1,000 marks i.e. £656.13.4. The King's gift however was not so very generous as it was found that the properties he had left for the purpose were in dreadful condition and therefore the whole of the cost actually fell on the City Corporation.

Nevertheless, Henry VIII still gets the credit of foundation and his statue (the only one in London) is over the gate. This is not contemporary because the gate was built in 1702. From the beginning, the hospital had its own chapel, St. Bartholomew the Less, where Inigo Jones was baptized in 1573. John Stow tells us of a number of brasses in existence and one still remains, that of William Markeby which has a curious erasure of part of the inscription. The part which reads 'May God be propitiated for their Souls' has been deleted, possibly by a Puritan Protestant. The chapel was rebuilt on an octagonal plan

62

in 1823 but many early memorials have been retained, including one to the wife of Thomas Bodley, the founder of the Bodleian Library at Oxford. A visit to this chapel and the Great Hall of the hospital can be made by arrangement with the Vicar and the authorities at the hospital.

Elsing Spital

The hospital known as 'Elsing Spital' on London Wall was also surrendered to Henry. It was founded by one William Elsing in 1332 for one hundred blind persons 'In honour of the Blessed Virgin Mary'. It was known as St. Mary Within Cripplegate. The building later became dwelling houses and a carpenter's yard.

The adjacent church of St. Alphege was pulled down and part of Elsing Spital became the parish church. This was closed in 1920.

The north wall of the first St. Alphege was part of the City Wall and for many years it has been exposed to view. The little that remains of Elsing Spital is 15th century work and is on view in London Wall (Street) making a remarkable contrast to the modern 'flat faced rent collecting slabs' which have arisen around it.

Bedlam

The Hospital of St. Mary of Bethlehem had been founded by Simon Fitzmary in 1247. In 1377 it was used for 'distracted persons' hence the term 'Bedlam' (a corruption of 'Bethlehem'). It stood 'without Bishopsgate' where Liverpool Street Station stands today. Broad Street Station booking office stands on the churchyard.

When he gave the care of St. Bartholomew's to the City Corporation, Henry also gave Bedlam into their care.

The hospital had always had benefactors who exhibited varying degrees of generosity. Edward III in 1329 gave the licence that allowed the inmates to beg, and then in 1375 seized the hospital as an 'alien Priory' because it was paying out 13/4 a year to a parent Convent in France.

At the beginning of the 15th century the treasurer pocketed all the funds and was later charged with stealing, among other things, four pairs of iron manacles, five chains of iron, and six chains with locks. It would seem that the brethren hadn't much faith in exorcisms!

A licence to beg made it possible for the less violent inmates to be allowed out on the street and the tin plate worn on the arm and exhibiting the five-pointed star of Bethlehem made 'Tom of Bedlam' a familiar sight to Londoners.

The opportunities thereby presented were not lost on the 'rowsey, ragged, rabblement of rakehells' who professed to have been in Bedlam and proceeded to cash in on the begging bit!

Such disreputables, when apprehended by the law, were punished by the 'House of Correction' at Bridewell by means of whipping posts, ducking stools, pillories and stocks.

In 1547, Bethlehem and Bridewell were placed under the same management.

In 1674 the buildings at Bishopsgate had become so dilapidated that the hospital was moved to a new site. Moorfields was chosen and the buildings stood along London Wall. The garden was the present Finsbury Circus. It was in these buildings that the cages for the inmates were arranged so that a visit to Bedlam to watch their antics became one of the sights of London. Later the hospital was moved again, this time to St. George's Fields and eventually to East Wickham, Kent.

The Lord Mayor, Sir Richard Gresham, appealed to Henry to allow the Corporation to take control 'of St. Mary Spital, St. Bartholomew, St. Thomas's and Tower Hill which were founded in London for the aid of the poor and wretched people and not to maintain canons, priests and monks to live in pleasure'.

Previous page: *The statue of John Snow in St. Andrew Under-shaft.* Above: *The model of the Royal Exchange in the London Museum.* Right: *Water runs down Lovat Lane, just like a gutter in a medieval or Tudor street*

Left: *The main entrance to Hampton Court with a bridge across the former moat.* Above: *Hampton Court, looking across Base Court towards the Anne Boleyn Gate and the Great Hall of Henry VIII*

Left: *Crosby Hall showing an Oriel window (Yevonde).*
Above top: *The great Bed of Ware which is in the Victoria and Albert Museum (Victoria & Albert Museum).* Above lower: *A dinner table of the time of Elizabeth I (Guildhall Museum)*

The statue of Queen Elizabeth I which is outside St. Dunstan-in-the-West, Fleet Street
All photographs are by Michael Taylor except where stated

Spitalfield Market now marks the site of St. Mary Spital, and the 'Tower Hill' referred to, the 12th century foundation in East Smithfield of St. Catherine's Hospital.

Throughout its existence it had enjoyed numerous Royal favours and even had a Charter for a twenty-one day Fair on Tower Hill. Henry VIII and Catherine of Aragon founded a Chapel there in 1526 and the hospital escaped dissolution, but it was destroyed to provide a site for St. Catherine Dock in 1825. Several relics of the Chapel were incorporated into St. Catherine's, Regent's Park.

St. Thomas's

St. Thomas the Martyr (Thomas Becket) was the original name of the hospital founded by the Canons of St. Mary Overie Priory in Southwark in the 13th century. All were surrendered to Henry VIII in 1538 and at that time the staff was a Master, six Brethren, and three Lay Sisters who looked after forty poor people. The City finally purchased the hospital for £647.4.1 and in 1553 King Edward VI granted a Charter to the City as Governors, but Henry VIII had stopped any reference to 'Thomas Becket'. The dedication became St. Thomas the Apostle.

Part of the chapel of the hospital in St. Thomas's Street, Bormondsey, now serves as the chapter house for St. Mary Overie, Southwark Cathedral, and in the attic of the tower can be seen the oldest operating theatre in England. Permission to visit it can be obtained from Guy's Hospital.

Other changes have also taken place since Queen Elizabeth's reign. At that time patients who did not behave were whipped or put in the stocks, and if they did not attend church on Sunday they lost their dinner. In those days even the nurses were sometimes whipped for bad behaviour, but some people would still favour the treatment for weak stomachs—it included one quart of ale for dinner and one pint for supper!

The End of the Friaries

The earliest foundations in and around London had been the monastic and hospital foundations, but at an early date the church itself had been aware that the austere rules of celibacy, chastity, abstinence, poverty, and prayer were not being fully observed, and took steps to restore the situation by the introduction of the friars. There were four orders, all of which were represented in London: Dominicans (Black friars) from 1221, Franciscans (Grey friars) from 1224, Carmelites (White friars) from 1241, and Augustinians from 1253.

The duties of monks were to provide hospitality to travellers, distribute alms to the poor, and say prayers for the founders, benefactors, and their heirs. To be able to do the first two, the monasteries had to have money and property.

The rules of the friars were similar but their duties were very different: not to distribute alms or provide hospitality, but to teach and pray. They were to move among the people and own nothing except the habit they wore. The church was well aware that poor people were more likely to believe in the teaching and prayers of a poor priest than those of a rich one.

The appeal of this form of popular religion could perhaps be regarded as an early form of revivalism and generally the friars were popular with people but disliked by the parish priests.

This popular appeal soon spread to the rich who corrupted the friars with gifts and influence. Continual close contact with the secular world also laid the friars open to all the temptations of the flesh and their original high purpose was degraded.

Consequently, by the time their turn came for dissolution the friaries were as corrupt as any of the religious houses, but in general they owned their friaries and not much else besides.

Greyfriars

The Greyfriars' (Franciscans) great church stood on the north side of 'The Shambles'—now Newgate Street, sometimes called 'Flesh Shambles' because of the great meat market stretching down the centre of the road. The western (Cheapside) end was called 'Blowbladder Street' and the street now named King Edward Street was 'Stinking Lane'.

The church, which was built in the early 14th century, stretched its 300 feet length from the City Wall by Newgate to Stinking Lane. The rest of the buildings consisted of the library (founded by Richard Whittington), Frator (dining hall), Dorter (dormitory), chapter house, a great cloister, little cloister, and domestic buildings. It covered the area now occupied by the G.P.O.

It has been said that 'no order of Monks had the power of persuasion equal to these poor Friars', and so strong was the desire to be wrapped in the grey woollen shroud of the friars when buried, that no less than 663 of the nobility, including four Queens, were buried in the building.

The insurance that could be arranged for the protection of the soul after death by the prayers of various Orders, was of major concern to most people and there were plenty of instances of backing two horses. Queen Eleanor (the wife of Henry III) was buried at Westminster (Benedictine) but her heart was buried at Greyfriars (Franciscan).

The choir of the Friary Church was named Christchurch and became the parish church. St. Nicholas Shambles (next door) was pulled down and all the parishes combined with that of St. Audeon—a church which had stood on the opposite side of the Shambles.

The rest of the buildings were granted to the City Corporation and the Lord Mayor bought the church monuments for £50. Christchurch was burnt in the Great Fire, rebuilt by Wren and all except the tower was destroyed in the blitz in the last war. The tower will remain but the church is not to be rebuilt, the graveyard on the west is part of the nave of Greyfriars Church.

As the result of a plea from the City Corporation, who were concerned with the vast number of orphans and poor children destitute and uncared for on the streets, Edward VI founded Christ's Hospital in 1553 and very soon three hundred and eighty orphans were received into it. Masters were installed and the school embarked on various activities to raise money. Boys were let out as mutes for funerals and for the drawing of lotteries, dressed in the long blue gown with yellow smock. Today they still wear the gown but with yellow stockings.

When the school moved to Horsham in 1902 some pieces of the Newgate Street buildings were also taken to Horsham and incorporated into the new buildings. Because of the City Corporation's interest in the school the scholars come to London once a year on St. Matthew's Day for tea in the Mansion House with the Lord Mayor. The visit is always an occasion in the City because the school band heads the procession from London Bridge Station to St. Sepulchre's Church, Holborn Viaduct. This is now used because Christchurch is a ruin. The original drawings of the school were damaged in the Great Fire, and were later partly rebuilt by Wren, but today the site is occupied by the G.P.O. and Bart's Hospital.

Blackfriars

The Blackfriars had arrived on the banks of the Fleet River in 1278, when they were given permission to break down the City Wall where it ran down from Ludgate to the Thames. Later, the City Corporation had to rebuild the wall round the outside of the Friary, but Edward I did give 100 marks (£33. 6. 8.) towards the cost!

On a number of occasions Parliament sat at Black-friars, various dignitaries including Emperor Charles V were lodged there, and the Legatine Court set up by the Pope for Henry VIII's proposed divorce was convened there.

In common with all the friaries it was surrendered in 1538 and the buildings were given to various people in favour at the time. Sir Thomas Carwardine received most of them, including the church cloisters, chapter house and churchyard.

In Queen Elizabeth's time the area became very fashionable and the Queen visited the Earl of Worcester and Lord Cobham there. The Earl and Countess of Somerset lived there in James I's reign together with such painters as Van Dyck and Cornelius Janson.

In 1596 James Burbage bought the Parliament Chamber and other buildings to create the second Blackfriars Theatre, William Shakespeare had a share in the later enterprise when the 'King's Men' as a syndicate of seven played there. Richard and Cuthbert Burbage (James's sons), William Sly, John Heminge, and Henry Condell. The last two were friends of Shakespeare, and collected and published the first folio after his death.

One play produced in this Theatre is especially worth mentioning. The play *Henry VIII* includes the scene of the Legatine Court and it was acted in the same hall that had seen this historical event only a few years before.

Many fragments of the original buildings can be seen at St. Dominic's Priory on Haverstock Hill in Hampstead where they were moved when St. Dominic's was established.

A walk around Blackfriars still discloses quite a lot of information about the friary. Start at the corner of Carter Lane and Blackfriars Lane, where a plaque states that the Blackfriars Priory stood here. Blackfriars Lane marks the western end of the church. Immediately behind the plaque on this north-western corner stood a Lady Chapel. Now walk eastwards up Carter Lane to Church Entry, you have now walked the length of the nave. Return to Blackfriars Lane and turn left (southward); when you reach the Apothecaries Hall on your left you have crossed the western end of the church. The Hall occupies part of the site of the porter's lodge and the guest house was alongside. The Hall was built after the Great Fire in 1670 but the Apothecaries Company were previously in Cobham House on this same site.

Turn left into Playhouse Yard. The Playhouse occupied the Parliament Chamber and that stood partially on this square. The King's printer worked here publishing the first *London Gazette* in 1666.

Continue to Church Entry on the left, which marks the east wall of the Great Cloister and the west end of the chapter house and certain domestic buildings. It also marks a line of division between the nave and the choir of the priory church.

The parish church of the friary precinct was St. Ann's —it was pulled down by Carwardine but later he had to build a substitute—St. Ann's Church, which was rebuilt over part of the Provincials Hall with the dorter and the infirmary cloister over it. St. Ann's was burnt in the Great Fire and not rebuilt, and the site was later used as a graveyard, together with another in Church Entry.

You have now reached Ireland Yard which gets its name from a tenant of this area even before William Shakespeare bought a house here in 1612. His Deed of Conveyance is at the Guildhall.

Whilst in this area it is worthwhile looking at two more places associated with Shakespeare. Continue eastward

BLACKFRIARS PRIORY

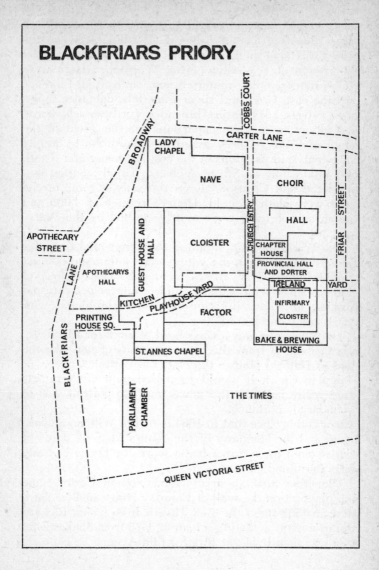

along Carter Lane and turn right into Wardrobe Court. Here from the time of Edward III till 1709, when the Office was abolished, stood the King's wardrobe under the charge of a 'Master of the Wardrobe'. Here were stored robes, clothes, materials, and cloths from Florence and the east. Gold and silver materials, damasks, tapestries, velvets, silks, satins, brocades, cords, tassels, barge decorations, and horse caparisons for the 'Field of the Cloth of Gold'. Wolsey asked the Wardrobe to supply some tents and pavilions in the costliest materials : 'Cloth of Gold, Cloth of Silver, Velvets, Tinsels, Satins embroidered and Crimson.' Even the sails of some of the ships were cloth of gold. Henry's retinue of 4,000 and Catherine's of 1,200 were mostly clothed by the Wardrobe.

The Wardrobe also supplied the ceremonial dress for Edward VI's coronation : white velvet jerkin and doublet trimmed with silver, rubies, diamonds, pearls, cloak of cloth of silver with damask gold; white velvet cap and buskins; and hose in crimson satin embroidered with pearls and damask gold.

The Wardrobe was always hard at work for Elizabeth, as can be seen from the many portraits of her, like the ones at Hatfield House, the National Portrait Gallery, or Hampton Court. It would seem that most of the artists were really painting the gown and the portrait was of secondary importance.

It was this office that in 1604 issued to William Shakespeare and the company of the 'King's Men' 4½ yards of scarlet cloth for a gown to be worn for James I's State entry into London.

The other Shakespearian connection in Carter Lane is a plate set on the wall of Faraday House at Bell Yard. Here in 1598 stood the Bell Tavern from which Richard Quincey wrote soliciting a loan of £30 from Shakespeare who was then living at Stratford on Avon.

Austin Friars

The Augustinians or Austin Friars were first founded in 1253 and when the priory was dissolved in 1538 Thomas Cromwell was one of the tenants. John Stow writes:

. . . namely, in Throgmorton Street, one very large and spacious, built in the place of old and small tenements by Thomas Cromwell, master of the king's jewel-house, after that master of the rolls, then Lord Cromwell, knight, lord privy seal, vicar-general, Earl of Essex, high chamberlain of England, etc., this house finished, and having some reasonable plot of ground left for a garden, he caused the pales of the gardens adjoining to the north part thereof on a sudden to be taken down; twenty-two feet to be measured forth right into the north of every man's ground; a line there to be drawn, a trench to be cast, a foundation laid, and a high brick wall to be built. My father had a garden there, and a house standing close to his south pale; this house they loosed from the ground, ere my father heard thereof; no warning was given him, nor other answer, when he spake to the surveyors of that work, but that their master Sir Thomas commanded them so to do; no man durst go to argue the matter, but each man lost his land, and my father paid his whole rent, which was 6s. 6d. the year, for that half which was left. Thus much of mine own knowledge have I thought good to note, that the sudden rising of some men causeth them to forget themselves.

The area was bounded by London Wall, Copthall Avenue, and Angel Court on the west, and Throgmorton Street and Broad Street on the east. The Church had been rebuilt in 1354 in Early Perpendicular Gothic style in such a manner as to warrant the statement that it was 'one of the beautifullest and rarest spectacles of the City'. It contained the tombs of several Plantagenets.

Thomas Cromwell's ill-acquired house and gardens reverted to the Crown on his execution and was bought by the Draper's Company in 1541. The hall they use today was rebuilt in 1870 but they still manage to retain one of the very few private gardens in the City, and they raise an annual crop of mulberries.

In 1547 the west end of the church was loaned to the Reformed Church from Germany and the Netherlands; and it later became the Dutch Church serving some 5,000 refugees in the area. Queen Mary expelled the Dutch in 1553 but they returned in 1559 under Queen Elizabeth. In 1518 under Henry VIII the funds of the Dutch community were seized but they managed to retain the Church. It was destroyed in the Second World War. On the 23rd July 1950 Princess Irene of the Netherlands laid the foundation stone of the fine church which stands there today.

The western wall of the friary can still be traced in the barrier wall in Draper's Garden along the south side of the new National Provincial Bank. Carpenters Hall at London Wall is on part of the northern boundary, and the entrance to Austin Friars from Old Broad Street marks the site of the main gate to the friary.

The Friars of the Blessed Virgin of Mount Carmel had their London foundation in 1241 between Fleet Street and the Thames. The friary was bounded on the north by Fleet Street and on the west by the Temple Wall and Sergeant's Inn. It extended to the Thames on the south and Whitefriars Street on the east. Some indication of the state of the Fleet river in 1290 is given by the fact that the friars complained that the stench rising from it overcame the scent of their incense. And the friary was at least 150 yards from the Fleet!

The friary was much used as a bank but suffered a shock in 1307 when, with the help of a friar 'Judas', thieves succeeded in stealing 40 pounds of silver. In 1538 the buildings were granted to a number of different people, Sir William Butts, Henry VIII's physician, gained most; he got the chapter house, the prior's lodging, 'The Olde Quere', the friar's dormitory, and the woodyard, for

74

all of which he had to pay a rent of 2/-. The house which Butts built was later granted to the Bishop of Worcester. The King's Armourer, Richard Morrison, gained the friar's library, Frator (dining hall), kitchen, some other buildings, and the garden. Another servant, Sir Richard Page, had the Provincial's Lodging and several others obtained various buildings and properties outside the friary.

Many cheap tenements were built in the area. And as these decayed they gave refuge to many criminals and fugitives from the law. In 1580 the inhabitants claimed to be exempt from the jurisdiction of the City and to enjoy the liberties as the friars had done before them.

Only one relic of the great friary remains, it is a cellar beneath the present buildings in Brittons Court, White-friars Street, built in the 14th century of hard white chalk blocks groined with eight stone ribs. It is some 3 feet below the present pavement level and once served as a Victorian Coal Cellar. The entrance to Bouverie Street at Fleet Street marks the site of the Greyfriars Great Gate and Pleydell Court is the site of the Friars Little Gate. Lombard Street runs alongside the friars' cemetery and the west end of the friary church, Temple Lane and Temple Avenue mark the garden. Tallis Street and Tudor Street were built across the garden. The friars' mill stood where Tudor Street meets Whitefriars. Bouverie Street was built through the middle of the church nave and across part of the cloister, Magpie Alley alongside the Dorter, Ashentree Court in part was over part of the cloister, and the crypt which has been found in Britton Court appears to have been under the prior's house.

Also included in the Dissolution were the large numbers of Chantries—religious establishments set up to pray for the soul of a benefactor—and the fine houses of the Abbots and Bishops. The latter were particularly common along the Strand.

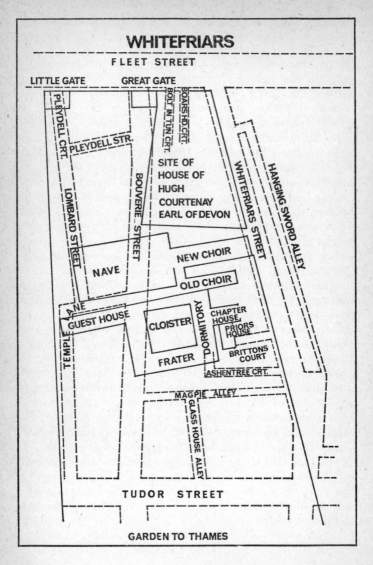

WHITEFRIARS

FLEET STREET

LITTLE GATE   GREAT GATE

PLEYDELL CRT.

PLEYDELL STR.

BOARS HD. CRT.

BOLT IN TUN CRT.

SITE OF
HOUSE OF
HUGH
COURTENAY
EARL OF DEVON

BOUVERIE STREET

LOMBARD STREET

WHITEFRIARS STREET

HANGING SWORD ALLEY

NAVE

NEW CHOIR

OLD CHOIR

TEMPLE LANE

GUEST HOUSE

CLOISTER

DORMITORY

CHAPTER HOUSE

PRIORS HOUSE

FRATER

BRITTONS COURT

ASHENTREE CRT.

MAGPIE ALLEY

GLASS HOUSE ALLEY

TUDOR STREET

GARDEN TO THAMES

Tudor St. Paul's

The Tudor St. Paul's was a very different building from the present one.

Then it was over 450 years old; the exact length is disputed, but it was probably 585 feet excluding portico, and it was certainly longer than the present building. The Nave was 104 feet wide and 93 feet high (Westminster Abbey is 101 feet), the tower was 285 feet, with a spire rising 489 feet above the ground. The Norman nave had large windows; and a magnificent Rose Window was the great feature of the east end. The choir had been rebuilt in the 13th and 14th centuries in much the same style as the east end crossing of Westminster Abbey. Over all towered the great spire, even higher than Salisbury Cathedral as we know it today. The church had an extensive crypt beneath it. In the south corner of the precinct stood a separate bell tower.

The precinct was surrounded by a wall with a great gate, this faced Bowyer Row which looked down the hill to Lud Gate, which was situated at the end of Old Bailey, facing down the hill toward the Fleet river. In the north-west corner of the precinct stood the bishop's palace. Near the end of the north transept stood the charnel and in two sides of the angle formed by the east side of the north transept and the north side of the choir was St. Paul's Cross with an open air pulpit. In Edward

VI's time this had a special gallery for a royal congregation.

The Duke of Somerset pulled down the cloister and charnel to provide room for his Somerset House in the Strand. The only relics of all this are to be found in St. Paul's Churchyard close to the present Church. These are part of the preserved foundations of the chapter house exposed on the south side of the nave.

A number of events took place at St. Paul's during the period, including the marriage of Prince Arthur and Catherine in 1501 which was followed by a great banquet in the bishop's palace.

St. Paul's School was established in the churchyard in 1509 by Dean Colet; the school was later removed to Hammersmith and very recently to Barnes. It is now administered by the Mercers' Company.

In the same year Henry VII's body came here and was later taken to Windsor to await the completion of his chapel at Westminster; Henry VIII's coronation procession passed the building.

In 1547 Edward VI, who was only 9 years old, saw a Spaniard slide head-first down a rope from the tower to entertain him on his way to his coronation. During the next year, as a further part of the Dissolution, the Rood was torn down and burnt (2 people were killed in the process); the cloisters and charnel house were taken down; and 500 tons of bones were taken to the 'Bonehill'—now Bunhill Fields. All the treasures of the Cathedral were seized and melted down for their gold.

Edward VI gave the Manor of Paddington to St. Paul's, but as he had taken it from Westminster Abbey he merely 'robbed Peter to pay Paul'. Afterwards all saying of Mass at St. Paul's was stopped, and in 1552 a new book of Common Prayer was introduced. After Mary's Coronation in 1553, the services returned to Latin and the ceremony of appointing a Boy Bishop for St. Nicholas' Day was reintroduced. All these great events called for special sermons from St. Paul's Cross.

In 1555 all the Bells of the Church were rung because of a rumour that Mary had given birth to a son but it turned out to be a false alarm.

There had always been abuses of the Cathedral, people loitered in the building to transact business, some pillars carried notices of situations vacant, some were centres for business bargains, and people took short cuts through the building. As early as 1386, the bishop had threatened excommunication for 'Buying and selling, throwing stones, shooting arrows, relieving nature or playing ball in or around the Cathedral', but by now people were wheeling handcarts through the building and carrying vessels of ale, great baskets of fish, flesh, and fruit, and leading horses and donkeys. The Lord Mayor's Proclamation against this had little effect. Taking 'A turn with the "Good" Duke Humphrey' in 'Paul's Walk' remained the 'in' thing for poorer aspirants to fashionable behaviour. The bishop gave up, he leased his palace out and went to live in his Fulham Palace.

The spire was struck by lightning in 1561 and the roof was badly damaged by fire. Despite Elizabeth's efforts the spire was never replaced but the roof was rebuilt.

When the Pope issued a 'Bull' calling Elizabeth a bastard and a heretic in 1570, John Felton was hanged in St. Paul's Churchyard for nailing the 'Bull' to the door of the Bishop's Palace.

Several lotteries were drawn at the west end of the church at this time to raise money to fight the Spaniards. When the Armada had been defeated there was a great service of thanksgiving.

Many notable men of the age were buried in the Cathedral—Nicholas Bacon, Earl of Pembroke, Sir Thomas Heneage, Philip Sidney, Sir Francis Walsingham and of course Elizabeth's 'Dancing Chancellor' Sir Christopher Hatton, Lord Keeper of the Great Seal, Lord Chancellor, and Knight of the Garter. He had a coat of arms of 64 'quarterings' on his tomb which was 25 feet high. When he died in 1591 he owed the Crown £40,000 and that no doubt was the reason Elizabeth was so adamant about getting some money from the Bishops of Ely.

Principally by his flattering behaviour to the Queen, Hatton had obtained the gate house, the courtyard, garden, and orchard of the Bishop of Ely's Palace in Holborn, for a residence. The garden was particularly splendid and the palace is often mentioned by historians and by Shakespeare.

Hatton Garden, Hatton Hall, Hatton Yard, Saffron Hill, Ely Place and Ely Court, all mark the area. Ely Court has the 1546 'Mitre Tavern' with the cherry tree in it which is supposed to have marked a corner of the estate. The Crypt of St. Etheldreda Church in Ely Place appears to have pre-Saxon work in the foundations.

Hatton obtained all this on lease for 21 years at a cost of one red rose for the Gate House and ten loads of hay and £10 per annum for the garden. He had obviously flattered the Queen with a purpose! He then attempted to get the whole palace, but the Bishop resisted. Queen Elizabeth decided Hatton should stay in residence until Ely paid back the money spent on the buildings. The Bishop died and his eventual successor continued the fight.

It is said, although there is some doubt about the facts, that Elizabeth wrote to Bishop Heton of Ely: 'I would have you to know, that I who made you what you are, can unmake you, and if you do not forthwith fulfil your engagements by God I will immediately unfrock you.'

After many long years of disputes and demolition during the Civil War, the land was bought by the Crown and a perpetual pension was given to the Bishop of Ely.

Parish Churches

The community centre of the parish was the church and throughout the Tudor period there were over 100 churches in the City alone. Of these the Great Fire claimed at least 84.

There are mementos dating from before the Great Fire in most of the City's Churches but the north-east corner of the City escaped the Fire and therefore a few churches from that area have been included here.

All Hallows Staining, Mark Lane: All that is left is the rebuilt Tower but there is a Norman Crypt beneath it brought here from Lambes Chapel in Monkwell Street. This street was near Cripplegate and it has been obliterated by the reconstruction of London Wall. On the corner of Markwell Street and Silver Street, William Shakespeare lived in 1604 at the house of Mountjoy, a theatrical costumier. The Public Record Office Museum in Chancery Lane exhibit a deposition signed by Shakespeare in 1612 relating to his lodging there.

St. Alphage, London Wall has some Tudor brick-work repairs to the City Wall, which supported the north wall of the church.

St. Andrew Undershaft has two particular points of interest; the name Undershaft is believed to come from the fact that on May Day each year until 1517 a Maypole, taller than the steeple of the church, was set up in Leadenhall Street outside the church. The Maypole was kept under the eaves of cottages opposite the church but in 1517 the Curate of St. Catherine Cree Church preached a sermon at St. Paul's Cross in which he stated that the Maypole was an idol. The London apprentices who were always ready to demonstrate, went in a body to St. Andrew's and pulled down the Maypole, cut it in pieces and burnt it. Unfortunately the apprentices, in the excitement, indulged in a riot of damage and looting, particularly aimed at foreigners. Many people were injured and the uproar continued all day and night. Eventually the City Aldermen got control but Wolsey, who always tended to interfere with City affairs, insisted on making an example of the apprentices. The City authorities were accused of losing control, and the rioters of committing treason. Despite strenuous efforts by Sir Thomas More, supported by the Lord Mayor and Aldermen, an unspecified number of the 'poore younglings' were executed. Later 400 men and boys and 11 women were paraded in Westminster Hall crying for mercy, with halters round their necks and dressed only in their shirts. They were treated to a long tirade and rebuke from Wolsey before the King, who was present in full state, granted them his pardon. This event was known as the 'Evil May Day'.

The other notable feature about St. Andrew's is its connection with John Stow the London historian who was buried there. He died on the 5th April 1605 and his widow erected a memorial of marble and alabaster, which takes the form of a carved figure of Stow writing in a book. Annually on a date near the anniversary of his death a Memorial Service is held, with the Lord Mayor and Sheriffs in attendance. After the service a new quill pen is placed in the hand of the figure and the old one removed. An essay competition between scholars of all London schools takes place before this event, and the writer of the best essay on London is given a prize copy of Stow's book, while the headmaster of the school concerned receives the old quill pen.

St. Botolph, Aldgate was rebuilt in 1744 but it contains a number of Tudor graves, including several from the executions on Tower Hill. Also, only shown on request, they have a mummified head which came there from Holy Trinity Minories when the two parishes were joined in 1909. An interesting dispute arose in connection with this head; the remains of the dissolved Abbey of The Minoresses of St. Clare were granted in 1552 to Henry Grey, Duke of Suffolk, father of Lady Jane Grey. He was executed in 1554, and one authority thought it was Grey's head. Later another scholar denied this story saying that in 1786 an infamous beadle had sawn up a lot of coffins to get the wood and 'had cut and slashed among the dead', thereby amputating a head!

St. Botolph's, Bishopsgate: Edward Alleyn was baptized here in 1566 and Ben Jonson's infant son was buried in 1600. Here also Sir Paul Pinder was buried; the façade of his great house which stood in Bishopsgate is preserved in the Victoria and Albert Museum. The railings of the Churchyard came from Old London Bridge but only small pieces remain. The church was rebuilt in 1729.

St. Ethelburga, Bishopsgate is an early 15th century church; the smallest in the City with later improvements and alterations. In the 16th century the Rector, John Larke, was a friend of Sir Thomas More and was helped by his influence. But later he was hanged at Tyburn because, together with Sir Thomas, he would not accept Henry as head of the church.

It was in this church in 1607 that Henry Hudson with his 13 year old son took their last Communion before sailing to discover Hudson's Bay.

St. Giles, Cripplegate was badly damaged in the last war. The Tower is 16th century with 17th century additions and most of the notable events connected with the church are post Tudor. However, it did once have a memorial window to Edward Alleyn who owned the 'Fortune Theatre' close by in Golden Lane, Barbican.

St. Dunstans in the West, Fleet Street, is on the west of the City and narrowly escaped the Great Fire, but the old building was demolished and a new church built in 1831. There is an interesting statue of Queen Elizabeth over the side porch and also, just inside the porch, the statues of 'King Lud and his two sons' all of which came off the old Lud Gate.

St. Margaret's, Westminster. The east window of this church is a quite remarkable survival from the period and 'survival' is an appropriate word. The window, which is Flemish in origin, was designed to go into the Henry VII Chapel at Westminster Abbey and was given to the Church by Catherine of Aragon's parents, Ferdinand and Isabella of Spain, to commemorate the wedding of their daughter to Prince Arthur who died 18 weeks later. By the time the window was finished Henry VIII was King and he had married the widowed Catherine. The left and right figures in the window depict the kneeling figures of Catherine and Arthur and were not the sort of reminder that Henry wanted, so the window was banished to Waltham Abbey. At the dissolution of the monasteries the window was sent to New Hall, Essex, where Ann Boleyn's father got hold of it. General Monk of the Parliamentarian army eventually acquired it and he buried it to protect it from Puritanical destruction. After the Restoration of Charles II the window was sold into private hands and later it was sold to St. Margaret's where it was installed at the east end of the church. It is now to be seen within about 200 feet of its original intended position.

The Tower and Tyburn

Henry VII followed the usual custom of the times and stayed at the Tower of London before his coronation on the 30th October 1485. While he was there he created twelve Knights of the Bath in the apartments adjoining St. John's Chapel in the White Tower. This Chapel was traditionally the one used for the creation of such knights, but they now use the Henry VII Chapel at Westminster. Four months later Henry married Elizabeth of York and she visited the Tower in 1487 when eleven more Knights of the Bath were created before her coronation.

In the meantime Henry had started the Tudor collection of prisoners in the Tower, the first one of note being Edward, Earl of Warwick, the unfortunate son of the dead Duke of Clarence. He was last in the male line of the Plantagenets and therefore a threat to the Tudors. For this reason, and apparently no other, at the age of 24 he was executed on Tower Hill in 1499. Twice during his reign Henry had to deal with Royal Pretenders, both alleged Plantagenets. The first was Lambert Simnel, who was brought to the Tower in 1487, but Henry showed mercy and simply made him a scullion in the Royal kitchen. The second, Perkin Warbeck, a more serious threat, was hanged at Tyburn, also in 1499. Tyburn, which had long been the central execution place of

London, was at the end of Tyburn Way. The unhappy route, along which criminals were taken on their last ride, was later called Oxford Street, and the dreadful associations of Tyburn itself were eliminated by the changing of its name to Marble Arch.

Throughout Tudor times the Tower was the centre of the nation's attention, it formed both stage and backcloth for some of the most moving events in English history.

The difference between the Tower and Tyburn as a place of execution was really only a matter of a person's degree or importance, and whether the event took place on Tower Hill and provided a day out for the Londoners, or whether it took place on Tower Green within the Tower, was a matter of policy, not necessarily determined by the sex of the victim. Executions by the sword instead of the axe could be reserved for Queens, as in the case of Ann Boleyn, whose execution was postponed for a day

Religious persecution: heretics being burned at Smithfield

in order to import the best man for the job. The unfortunate 70-year-old Countess of Salisbury, however, had only an axeman, and an inferior deputy at that—three of the more experienced ones having themselves been executed not long before at Clerkenwell. Suffice it to say therefore that twelve men and five women of some notability were executed on Tower Hill from the beginning of Henry VII's reign to the death of Elizabeth, but many more humble people were executed elsewhere, for instance the Babbington Plotters were beheaded in Lincoln's Inn Fields.

In between the long sequence of executions Henry VIII built the Lieutenants' Lodgings, now called the Queen's House, which is the only access to the Bell Tower. This made that tower a very secure prison. In 1512 the 400 year old Chapel of St. Peter ad Vincula (St. Peter in Chains) was burnt out and then rebuilt.

Elizabeth's name became associated with the roof leads between the Bell Tower and Beauchamp Tower which was known as 'Elizabeth's Walk' after she had taken exercise there during her imprisonment by Mary.

There is another 'Elizabeth's Walk' at Windsor Castle but she had that one built herself.

Many of the prisoners of the period left their marks on the walls of the various Towers which held them prisoner, especially the Dudley brothers in the Beauchamp Tower, and Sir Walter Raleigh who is remembered in another roof exercise area by the Bloody Tower.

The journey to 'go west' generally started at Newgate jail when, if they were not to be 'drawn' (dragged at the tail of a cart) on a litter, they went 'in the cart' sometimes standing beside their own coffin but always accompanied by an exhorting priest. Some form of exhortation to repent their sins was met at nearly every church they passed, but at St. Giles in the Fields they received the extra cheer of a bowl of ale. The Angel Tavern near the church provided this and became known as 'The Bowl'.

The first date at which Tyburn is mentioned is 1177 and it was used for executions until November 1783. It has been estimated that in those 600 years at least 50,000 people died there. This is less than 100 a year, but the rate accelerated violently in Tudor times to about 224 a year.

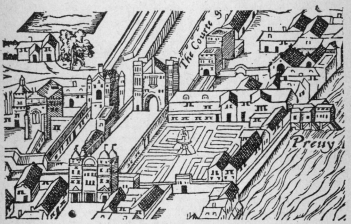

The Palace of Whitehall in 1560

Lawyers

Staple Inn is the Tudor timber façade in Holborn opposite the end of Gray's Inn Road and standing across the City boundary. It helps us to visualise how most of London looked throughout the Tudor period. These buildings were erected between 1545 and 1589 and now have been preserved by rebuilding the houses behind, thereby supporting the frontage. You can see many of the features common to this form of building; oriol windows, some more shallow than others, with characteristic overhang at the extreme right hand end, and a double overhang in the centre. The left side is symmetrical having five gable ends with a stone arch in the centre. Unfortunately the Hall which had been built in 1581 was badly damaged during the war but it has now been restored and is occupied by the Society of Actuaries. In 1529 it was a Law School under the control of Gray's Inn and had 145 students in term and 69 out of term.

The gateway to Lincoln's Inn from Chancellors (Chancery Lane) was built in 1518 and has recently been substantially rebuilt. The Society of Lincoln's Inn used the Hall of the Bishop of Chichester's Palace until 1489. A little of the replacement Hall which was erected in 1489–91 still remains as it was used.

At the bottom of Chancery Lane in Fleet Street stands the entrance gate to Inner Temple, the original building was a Tavern called 'The Hand' and was built in 1610. It went through a series of tavern names, became a wax works and later a barber's shop. The front of the building was found to have had a false screen erected across it and when this was removed the ancient work was found to be in excellent condition. The upper room has a remarkable plaster ceiling, one of the best decorated Jacobean examples left in the City. The centre of the design contains the Prince of Wales's Feathers with the letters P.H., and it seems very likely that this may have been originally the Council Chamber of Prince Henry. Henry was James I's eldest son who was created Prince of Wales in 1610 (the first Prince of Wales for 100 years). At one time this building was 'The Prince's Arms' and the decoration and the name suggests that it could in fact be associated with Prince Henry. The Chamber is now controlled by the Greater London Council.

The Middle Temple Hall was opened in 1576 by Queen Elizabeth. It is 100 foot long, 40 foot wide, and 50 foot high. It is panelled throughout with a remarkable display of the arms and names of Readers and Treasurers painted on it. It contains some fine heraldic glass dating back to 1540, a table which was donated by Queen Elizabeth, and a serving table believed to have been made from timber of Drake's ship *The Golden Hinde*. The most remarkable feature of the Hall is the carved wooden screen, complete with a Minstrels' Gallery. This did suffer severe damage during the war and has been literally pieced together and replaced.

It was in this Hall that the first performance of *Twelfth Night* was given, but it is doubtful whether the suggestion that Queen Elizabeth was present is true. An interesting feature of the screen is the beautifully carved doors which were fitted in 1609 after the students of the Inn had forcibly taken possession of the Hall for several days so that they could celebrate Christmas festivities, which had previously been forbidden. The doors are furnished with decorative iron spikes to discourage climbers—most things, even students' 'sit-ins' have happened in London's past!

Southbank

From the south, the entry to London was along 'Long Southwark' and 'The Borough'. You passed St. George's Church on the right (east) which was almost alongside the prison of the Earl Marshal—known as The Marshalsea. The Earl Marshal originally had jurisdiction for 12 miles around the King's Court wherever it was. This prison ranked second only in importance to the Tower of London, and later it became a prison for debtors.

On the west side was the Court of the King's Bench and 'The Mint' which was a semi-official sanctuary. It was this area which is now bounded by Southwark Bridge Road, Southwark Street and the Borough that contained the houses of 'Minters' who were considered to be under the rule of the King's Bench Prison which was situated close by to the south. Any fugitive from the law might find sanctuary here in the warren of tenement houses. The inhabitants of all sanctuaries developed a slang language of their own, which in part still survives in mutilated form, in criminal slang today. For instance, the Elizabethan slang for poor imitation jewellery was 'Phawney', it was taken to America and has come back to us as 'Phoney'.

Several contemporary writers have mentioned the 'Mint'. John Gay in 'Beggar's Opera', Henry Fielding in 'Jonathan Wild' and Defoe in 'Moll Flanders'. The Mint was abolished in 1723 by a law which relieved all debtors under £50. These places have left us memories in Marshalsea Road and Mint Street.

Opposite St. George's Church was the sumptuous house of Charles Brandon, Duke of Suffolk, who was the husband of King Henry VIII's sister Mary. The house was surrounded by Orchards, Vineyards and Ponds, and Henry, in 1537, lent it to Campeggio the Papal Legate. When Henry debased the coinage between 1542 and 1549 he set up a coinage Mint here, and it was then renamed Southwark Place. The traveller to London then came into a long continuous market street full of Taverns and Inns on both sides. The traffic in both directions was enormous despite the stalls and street traders.

In the early part of the period bands of Pilgrims setting out for Canterbury, could be seen, especially early in the morning, and they often made their first stop at the well of 'St. Thomas a Watering' in Old Kent Road. Today it is still a stopping place as it has the tavern of St. Thomas à Becket on the same spot. The pilgrims had provided one of the reasons why 'Long Southwark' and 'The Borough' had such a profusion of inns.

At night, when curfew sounded, the Bridge Gate was closed until morning and anyone arriving late had to find accommodation outside it. If you intended to travel south from London you had to leave the City before curfew the night before, and stay overnight in Southwark so you could make an early start in the morning.

The sites of many of the Buildings and Taverns have been carefully marked since the war by the Southwark Authorities and they include the 'White Hart', which Jack Cade used as his headquarters when he lead the Peasants' Revolt on Sunday, 5th July 1450.

There is 'The Tabard' now named 'The Talbot' made famous by Chaucer, and 'The George', part of which still stands in a railway warehouse yard. This is a particularly appropriate connection because The George was always a carriers' inn. Carriers made up a very large part of the itinerant population of Southwark. As the city grew, the demand for supplies caused much congestion on the road and the existence of much chaos at the one bridge. There was also 'The White Lion' which became the County Gaol in the 16th century, and 'The Cross Keys' later called 'The Queen's Head' which was owned by a butcher whose son John Harvard became the founder of Harvard University.

As one approached The Bridge Gate through 'The Borough' the Pillory stood in the centre of the road by St. Margaret's Church which was opposite the 'George Tavern'. St. Thomas's Hospital and St. Olave's Church were on the right and St. Mary Overie (Over the Water) and the Bishop of Winchester's Palace with its 'Clink' Prison and 'Liberty' were on the left (west).

At the southern end of the bridge on the east you find Tooley Street—which is a corruption of St. Olave becoming 'Stoolave' then 'Stooley'. Pepper Alley ran to the west at Montague Close, between the river and the Priory of St. Mary Overie. This priory on the site of a 9th century (or earlier) nunnery and a college of secular priests had been refounded in 1106 as a College of Canons of the order of St. Augustine. It was here that John Gower, Chaucer's friend and Poet Laureate for Richard II spent his last days. In 1540 it was dissolved and together with a chapel called 'St. Mary Magdalene', was combined with the parish of St. Margaret's (mentioned above, and called St. Saviour's).

In 1545 the priory lands were given to Sir Anthony Browne, Master of Horse to Henry VIII. His son became Viscount Montague—Montague Close ran through the priory cloister, hence 'Close' where he built a house. St. Saviour's was rented by the parishioners from the Crown but fell into bad disrepair and Stow says that it 'was leased and let out and the House of God made a Bakehouse . . . in this they have their ovens . . . in that their kneading trough, in another (I have heard) a hogs' trough, for the words that were given me were these: *This place have I known a hog-stie, in another a store-house to store up their hoarded meal and in all of it something of this sordid kind and condition'.*

In Queen Mary's reign many heretics and clergy were tried in the Lady Chapel by Bishop Gardiner and Bishop Bonner, and later these prisoners were burnt at Smithfield. The parishioners bought this church from James I but after several restorations, repairs, and renovations, it was again neglected and for nine years in the 19th century the nave had no roof. At the end of the last century it was largely rebuilt and became Southwark Cathedral in 1905.

Among a number of notable burials in the Cathedral will be found Edmund Shakespeare (William's brother), John Fletcher and Philip Massinger. These two collaborated with William Shakespeare in writing *Henry VIII* which was produced at the Globe in 1613. The performance on the 2nd July wasn't completed because the over-enthusiastic firing of cannons by the 'effects' man set fire to the thatched roof and burned the Globe to the ground. The audience were lucky to escape. There was

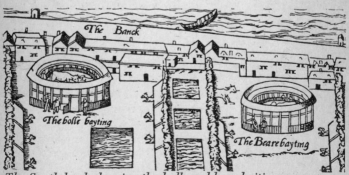

The South bank showing the bull- and bear-baiting arenas

one casualty—one man's breeches took fire but somebody saved his dignity with a can of beer! Also buried there is Lionel Lockyer who sold pills 'made from the rays of the sun to be an antidote against London fogs'.

Moving westward along the river today you will find St. Mary Overie Dock beyond the Cathedral, at the entrance to Clink Street. This is mentioned in the Domesday Book as a 'Harbour' and at one time it extended to the west gate of the priory. Parishioners could land goods here without charge.

Continuing along Clink Street on the left stood the great hall of Winchester House, the Palace of the Bishop of Winchester. One gable end of the wall is still standing supporting the end of a warehouse. Winchester Square was the courtyard of the palace. It is said that it was here that Catherine Howard was first brought to the notice of Henry VIII by the scheming Howards.

The park of the palace extended the length of Bankside to what is now Blackfriars Road, the riverside was built over and much of the property which was taverns, stews, or brothels, belonged to the bishop. Many of the brothel keepers, procuresses, and 'Bawds' were Flemish women and were called 'Winchester Geese' by Shakespeare.

From the 13th century Southwark had become a place of refuge for the City's outcasts and vagrants who were living in conditions of squalid poverty under the less strict control of the Surrey Magistrates. In 1550 it became a Ward of the City and a stone in the churchyard defines the boundaries. Since 1406 the City had exercised control over Southwark Market by way of the assay and assize of bread, victuals, and wine but control was never exercised as strictly as it was on the other side of the bridge and gradually the City's control was eroded away by the county authorities. The railway bridge marks Bank End and from here all along the river front were taverns, stews, brothels, and variations on the same theme, which increased the entertainment of the visitors from across the water, who came to see the plays, bear baiting, and cock fighting, or simply to have fun.

Curiously two names from the past remain, almost completely marking the extent of the Bankside of the period—'The Anchor' tavern at the eastern end still operates in a modernised building and Cardinal Cap Alley is on the site of a particularly notorious brothel at the western end beyond Southwark Bridge. In between stood 'The Gun', 'Castle', 'Bullhead', 'Crane', 'Beerpot', 'Vine', 'Elephant', 'Sugar Loaf', 'Three Tuns', 'The Bear', and 'The Barge', and there were many other taverns in alleys and streets running back from the river. Rose Alley marks the site of the Rose Theatre and just to the west was erected 'The Hope' in 1614. Bear Garden leads to the site of the bear pit which in 1594 was controlled by Edward Alleyn, 'The Master of the Royal Game of Bears, Bulls and Mastiff Dogs.' The base of this building is still recognisable in the positioning of the modern buildings.

The French ambassador was brought here by Queen Elizabeth in 1599 and later confessed he enjoyed it more than a visit to Westminster Abbey!

As a partnership, Edward Alleyn and Philip Henslowe had very substantial interests on Bankside, starting with 'The Rose' and later extending to the bear garden. Their property included many tenements, the 'Barge', the 'Bell and Cock', and stew houses and brothels. Not only was Alleyn a man of property, he was also possibly the best actor of his time. Before he died he had founded some almshouses, which were later moved to Dulwich, and in 1614 'The College of God's Gift' at Dulwich, where he is buried in the chapel.

The site of the Globe Theatre is now covered by the Courage Brewery and is marked by a plaque on the wall in Park Street. The story of the Globe's arrival on Bankside is interesting. The first Royal Patent for the 'Earl of

Leicester's Company' was issued in 1574. James Burbage was the chief actor and a joiner by trade; he erected 'The Theatre' in Shoreditch in 1576, for the City Corporation would not allow 'vagabond actors' in the City. The 'Wooden O' is therefore principally his design and later buildings were similar in plan.

Shortly afterwards another theatre was built nearby and this was called 'The Curtain'. Curtain Road, Shoreditch, marks the site, and several actors were buried in Shoreditch church.

In 1596 the lease for 'The Theatre' ran out and in the same year James Burbage died. His sons—Cuthbert and Richard—could not agree with their landlord and, with the assistance of Peter Streete, a master carpenter, they dismantled 'The Theatre', carried the timber across the river and re-erected the building close to the Rose, renaming it 'The Globe'. William Shakespeare had a one-tenth interest in this venture, and the Globe became 'the glory of the Bank'.

Early playactors were regarded as vagrants and consequently were continually being chased by parish constables and magistrates. The only protection they could get was by obtaining the patronage of some powerful person. There were no actresses, and women's parts were played by young men and boys. They usually travelled about the country giving shows in the open air, but the construction of inn yards made them the best stopping places.

Inns were often built around four sides of a courtyard with the inner sides of the building carrying external balconies and stairways. These balconies were ready-made viewing galleries for any action taking place in the courtyard below; therefore by arrangement with the tavern landlord, the actor's cart could be drawn into the yard and the tailboard would be used as a stage. The yard became the 'pit' from which 'the groundlings' could view the play while one of the company went round with a box to make a collection. We still buy our tickets at the 'Box office'.

These scenes are now re-acted at the 'George' in the Borough on Saturday afternoons in the summer.

Interior and exterior of 'The Globe', the best known Eliza-bethan theatre at which some of Shakespeare's plays were acted. The upper drawing shows the projecting stage with the audience seated all round it

The Bridge

It was always called 'The' Bridge because it was the only one, although today it is hard to realise that from the time of the earliest settlements on the banks of the Thames until 1729, the successive bridges on this site had been the only means of crossing the river in the London area, as far as Kingston; other than by going over by boat. In 1485 the bridge had already been in use over 300 years and it was going to stand there for nearly 350 more before it was finally replaced by the one which has now been sold to America.

The bridge was the most important street in Tudor London and only a few years earlier it had played a defensive role in one episode of the final stages of the Wars of the Roses.

King John, in 1209, had been the first to suggest putting houses on the bridge so that the rents would help with its upkeep; and Edward I had authorised the Mayor to take tolls from all who crossed it and from all ships that passed through the raised drawbridge. He also put the proceeds from the rents of the stalls on the 'Stock Market' which stood on the site of the present Mansion House, towards the upkeep of the bridge. One gory sight was that of traitors' heads on poles on the gatehouse to the bridge, one of the first heads of which to appear was that of William Wallace in 1305.

It was the healthiest place to live in London. In 1349 the 'Black Death' had killed about half of the population of the country and in 1665 bubonic plague carried off nearly 40 per cent of the population of London. But from both epidemics only two deaths are recorded among the people living on the Bridge.

A large open sewer ran underneath it into which everything was dumped—it is true it then washed up and down with the tide but it was felt that the Thames was big and wide enough to absorb this refuse without contamination. If you didn't trust the water you fished up in a bucket you could always tip it back and buy some from a water carrier, but you didn't know where he had got it from. After 1558 it may well have come from a conduit in Grasschurch Street (Gracechurch today) which was being supplied by pumps, worked by waterwheels fixed in the first arch of the northern end of the bridge and so it was Thames water anyway.

There were far more deaths caused by crushes in the traffic on the bridge, for it was only 20 foot wide at its widest and this came down to about 12 foot where there were houses and shops. The roadway was later widened to 20 foot by making the houses overhang the river. Between 1756 and 1762 all houses were removed and the bridge was widened to a width of 46 foot. Deaths by drowning were much more serious. In the 600 years of its life, it has been estimated that over 10,000 lost their lives: 'London Bridge was built for wise men to go over and fools to go under.'

To protect the twenty piers from the tide race, islands called 'Starlings' were built round them which made the piers look as if they were standing on great flat boats. These 'Starlings' further narrowed the water channels under the nineteen arches and increased the tide race so much, that there was often a 5 foot drop in the water level, no matter which direction the tide was running.

Wolsey and many others would never go under it and Queen Elizabeth also preferred to avoid going over it! The traders in the late 16th and 17th centuries gained most commercially as the bridge was a famous shopping centre.

A number of alterations were made to the bridge, between 1500 and 1600. By 1500 the stone gate which had been built in 1428 was so weak that the drawbridge could not be raised. After 1500 it does not appear to have been used at all, consequently the 'Bridge House' lost the 6d. toll it had previously been able to charge all ships passing through.

In 1504 there was a fire at the north end which burnt out six houses by St. Magnus the Martyr church. This church in Lower Thames Street is now screened from the present bridge by Adelaide House. It used to stand alongside the footway to the old bridge which was 100 feet east of the present one. Fish Street Hill (the lower end was called New Fish Street and the upper end Fish Street Hill in Stow's time) was the main road to and from the bridge for over 600 years and it wasn't any wider than it is today. After Christopher Wren had rebuilt the church which had been destroyed in the Great Fire, a footway was provided underneath the church tower to improve access to the bridge.

In 1535 Henry VIII ordered the rededication of all shrines bearing the name of Becket, and the chapel which stood on the ninth pier from the north and which had been the burial place of Peter of Colechurch, the builder of the bridge, was renamed the 'Chapel of our Lady'. In 1553 the Chapel was turned into a grocer's shop and leased to one William Bridger; its Gothic exterior was destroyed.

In the following year Sir Thomas Wyatt attempted to depose Mary Tudor and prevent her marriage to Philip of Spain. The bridge was put into a state of defence against the force, said to be 10,000 strong, that Wyatt was leading up from Kent. The drawbridge which was joined to the fourteenth arch (from the north) was 'hewen downe into the Thames' and 'rampiers and fortifications' were armed 'with great ordinance'. Householders had to close their shops and had to be armed at their doors ready for the fight, but when Wyatt realised the determination of the Londoners to resist him, he moved his force up river and crossed at Kingston. He finally capitulated after desultory skirmishes at Hay Hill, Mayfair, and along Fleet Street and Ludgate Hill.

The drawbridge gate was demolished in 1577 after all the heads on poles had been carefully transferred to the great stone gate at Bridge-foot (Southwark end) and foundations were prepared for what was to become the most remarkable building ever erected on the bridge.

This was 'Nonsuch House' a timber building four storeys high which had been partly prefabricated in Holland. It was fixed together with wooden pegs and without the use of one single nail. It had copper sheathed towers—turretted, onion domed, and ornamentally decorated; it also had an abundance of windows, in fact from some aspects it appeared almost all glass. It was painted in stone green and white, with a gilded weathervane and panelled coats of arms with supporters, and it took two years to complete. The drawbridge was abandoned and a permanent arch was built in its place.

The last arch at the south end was filled with a water wheel in 1559 to provide more power for the cornmill which was already in existence there.

In 1582 Sir Christopher Hatton, Queen Elizabeth's 'Dancing Chancellor', supported an application by Peter Morrice for permission to install waterwheels in the two northernmost arches to pump water into the City.

Unfortunately there are very few relics of this piece of London history to be seen today. In 1921 the second arch from the north end of the old bridge was exposed 'in situ' where it had remained under the building which had been erected when the new bridge was built in 1880; but it proved impossible to raise sufficient enthusiasm and £7,000 to preserve it.

All that is left of the old bridge is a few sections on the roof of Adelaide House and some pieces in the church-yard of St. Magnus the Martyr.

The section of the bridge in front of the church was known as 'The Square'. When the bridge was widened railings were placed round this area. Some of these went to the churchyard of St. Botolph Without Bishopsgate and pieces of them are still there, but evidently the men collecting iron railings for the war effort were not told their history because only very small pieces are left supporting one or two lamps.

The stone shelters were dispersed, one is in the court-yard of Guy's Hospital and two more are in Victoria Park in East London.

The bridge has, however, left us one other very tangible asset—'The Bridge House Estates'. While the bridge existed various people left money and properties for its upkeep, the rents and tolls seldom proved sufficient for the upkeep of the bridge. These funds are handled by 'The Bridge House Estate Committee' of the City Corporation and through them properties are managed and developed, and funds invested. The income has been continuously devoted to the upkeep of all City bridges: Blackfriars, Southwark, London, and even Tower Bridge. The latter is by far the most expensive. The cost of these bridges does not fall on the ratepayers of the City or other boroughs concerned. Furthermore sufficient reserves have been accumulated to enable the Bridge House Estates to undertake the rebuilding of the present London Bridge.

Life in Tudor London

Markets

London had always been a city of commerce, and there was now a great advance in economic planning and trading efficiency, as capital became available for bulk buying.

Wholesaling, called 'Regrating' or 'Forestalling' at the beginning of the period, was forbidden by the Guilds, and also by the City authorities. They regarded this form of activity in the way that we now regard the potential monopolist. With grain supplies fluctuating with the seasons and civic storage facilities being something of a gamble because of damp and vermin, individual 'forestalling', buying cheaply and selling for high prices, was almost a criminal activity. But as both the population and the demand increased so supplies had to come from further afield and in larger quantities.

Until the Civil War in the middle of the 17th century, the City successfully resisted the establishment of other markets outside the City Liberties, and thereby the pressure within the City increased.

Westward from Cheapside stretched the 'Shambles', one long meat market occupying the length of what is now Newgate Street. At the eastern end of Cheapside was Poultry with its own market, and Bucklebury with its grocers' stores filling the air with the more pleasant smell of their spices. Eastwards, along the length of

Cornhill, on the right was the Stocks—a market for fish and meat with some stalls clustered round the 'stocks' that stood there. This market developed fruit, vegetable, and floral sections.

Sir Thomas Gresham's Exchange was begun in 1566 and opened in 1570 by Queen Elizabeth who promptly dubbed it 'Royal'. Because English traders were now developing increasing interest in overseas markets, they needed a building in which they could meet and conduct business.

Before then one of the main business centres had been the nave of St. Paul's. The Royal Exchange was planned with shops around the outside of a quadrangle, the rents paying for its upkeep. The centre area was open to the sky and the 'Golden Grasshopper' weathervane was a permanent reminder of the man who built it at his own expense. Gresham's Exchange was burnt out in the Great Fire of 1666 and the new building was also burnt down in 1838. Both earlier buildings had their entrance on Cornhill. Only the floor survives from the original building.

An early Tudor woodcut of a housewife bargaining in a market

There was no market on Cornhill until one reached the junction of Leadenhall and Grasschurch Street, and came to stalls and pavement hawkers spilling out from Leadenhall Market. This was a 'foreign' market permitted by the City Corporation and mostly used by country poulterers.

From here, turning south down Gracechurch Street one next came to the Butchers' stalls of Eastcheap, which extended from Philpot Lane to Clement Lane (off Canon Street).

This street continued as New Fish Street which was where the Fishmongers gathered. Queenhithe (Queen's Harbour) was another centre for fishmongers and in Upper Thames Street the market area is still very clearly defined in modern building layout. This is one of the oldest harbours in London and was first mentioned in 899 in a charter of King Alfred. In the 13th century it was used for landings of corn and foreign fish, and later it was developed into a quay for handling foreign imports.

Stow tells us that garlic was sold in the market and this may account for the name of the church nearby—St. James Garlickhythe (Garlic Harbour) and the street, Garlick Hill.

Billingsgate was originally a market for coal and corn arriving by boat. It did not become a fish market until 1699.

Smithfield, since the 11th century, had been famous for its horse fair, but the Central Meat Market itself did not come into being until the City Corporation put a stop to the slaughter of cattle in the Shambles (Newgate Street) in 1614. All the slaughtering was then done at Smithfield until 1869 when the Shambles meat market was closed.

Sanitation

The healthiest people in Tudor and Elizabethan London were those living on the Bridge or those who had a house overlooking one of the river ditches or streams. The privies could be built out over these ready-made open sewers, and until they became blocked up with rubbish, life was fairly comfortable. The upper part of the Walbrook was covered over in 1440 but in Elizabethan times the end near the Thames was still open.

It was much more unpleasant to live in a street away from these primitive amenities. Household cesspits, often shared, were not usually cleaned out often enough. It was certainly common for chamber pots to be emptied out of the windows into the street. The gulley in the centre of the street was often choked with rubbish which the rakers had not removed. There were orders for all who had water supplies to flush the gullies daily but the general water supply was totally inadequate. The ultimate disposal of the rubbish was also inadequate, as it was taken to City 'laystalls' on the riverside and then removed in boats, to be finally dumped over the side where it was simply washed up and down by the tide. The streams and rivers were almost as foul as the ditches. Quite often casual labour was recruited for cleaning them and many regulations were made, but these were of little use because there was nobody to see they were carried out.

From the 14th century there had been at least one public latrine provided in each City Ward and scavengers had to see that these were kept in working order. A common failing was what happened near Baynard's Castle where it was complained that 'it was very ruinous because watermen had been fastening their boats to one of the posts and it had become very shaky'. Lord Mayor Richard Whittington in the 15th century had a very fine 30 seater latrine built at his own expense in the 'Vintry', at the north end of Southwark Bridge.

When it comes to the disposal of rubbish, Londoners have only changed the type of refuse that they throw into ponds, rivers, canals, or leave in fields and hedgerows. In Tudor and Elizabethan times it was 'dead dogs, cats, whelps, and kitlings.'

Speaking of Rither Lane, Billingsgate, Stow says it was 'now called Pudding Lane because the butchers of Eastcheap have their scalding house for hogs there, and their puddings with other filth of beasts, are voided down that way to their dung boats on the Thames'.

The effect on health was not understood. Londoners only knew that it was a nuisance and it stank. The word 'Pudding' is a middle English word used in the sense of bowels, entrails, and guts. It is possible that the Lane got its name for the reasons stated by Stow because in 1402 the butchers of Eastcheap had been given the right to 'build a bridge' (meaning a quay) so that they could throw their offal into the Thames at ebb tide. The area was also well known for the large number of 'Ordinaries' (cook shops) that served the growing working population who were involved in supplying ships.

London water was distributed from the conduits by water carriers, who in Tudor times founded the Brotherhood of St. Christopher of the Water Bearers. The wealthy members of society with great houses could sometimes have a 'quill' fitted. This was a small branch pipe from the main conduit supply.

In 1581 the City signed a 500 year lease to a Dutchman Peter Morrice—one of Sir Christopher Hatton's servants —which gave him the right to pump water from London Bridge to Leadenhall. In return for 10/- a year, and with the help of a water wheel in the northernmost arch of London Bridge, Peter Morrice supplemented the inadequate water supplies from the conduits.

In 1584 another similar scheme was developed at Broken Wharf, Thames Street. The Morrice family retained their interest until 1701 when they sold out to Richard Soames for a figure between £36,000 and £38,000. The two schemes were then combined to form a company. Eventually the company was taken over by the Metropolitan Water Board who still pay £3,750 per annum by way of annuities to the interested parties, and the Metropolitan Water Board will continue to pay until 2082 when Morrice's original 500 year lease is up. Although the fine conduit, which was set up at the corner of Leadenhall Street, served to wash down the channel of Bishopsgate, Cornhill, Leadenhall, and Grasschurch Street, and although many private houses were supplied with quills all the way up Grasschurch Street, this water supply was totally inadequate for the requirements of the City.

The best progress in obtaining supplies was made with the construction of the new river by Sir Hugh Myddleton at the end of the 16th century. In Canonbury a public garden runs alongside the water. He ran out of money through fighting law suits brought against him by the water bearers, and eventually King James I agreed to help him, provided he could have half of the profits. The work was completed in 1613. New River Head, Roseberry Avenue, in Clerkenwell, became the headquarters of the Metropolitan Water Board and the building occupies the site of the pond into which the 'New River' ran. Charles I sold back the Royal interest to Myddleton for a perpetual annual annuity of £500 and it became known as the 'King's Clog'. William IV gave it away for the payment of a debt, but the Metropolitan Water Board still pay their rents annually.

In addition to all these schemes there were a number of wells in use in the City to boost the water supplies. Well Court, off Queen Street, just north of Queen Victoria Street, was named because no less than twenty-two wells of Roman origin have been discovered in the immediate vicinity. The northern part of the Fleet River (north of Holborn Viaduct) which still runs under Farringdon Road, was known as the River of Wells, and Stow lists about four or five, most of which were renowned for the entertainments that took place at certain times of the year. Many other wells and conduits were spread over the City and they were fed from various sources. The cesspools, over-crowded churchyards, ditches, puddles, and ponds all drained into the wells or rivers, so that conduit water was being pumped from the same river that eventually received all the effluent from the lay-stalls and dung heaps.

It was fortunate that nearly everybody drank beer from a very early age. At least the water had been boiled!

Clothing and Fashions

Men and women continually wore clothes which were intended to alter their figures, by the skilful use of padding and frameworks. All were made in rich fabrics with bright colours, often varying in length or draped to show another rich material underneath.

Ladies' gowns were full skirted and touched the ground, they were often braided and embroidered, and open from the waist downwards to display an equally rich underskirt. They had vee or square necklines, sometimes very wide, and often very full sleeves.

The 'Farthingale' was developed from a stiff canvas petticoat to become a whalebone-stiffened undergarment with hoops of varying sizes to produce a cone shape which accentuated a small waist.

Later, padded shoulders, sometimes like large epaulettes, were finished with very puffed sleeves, and the skirt hoops were made wider at the top, eliminating the hoops lower down the frame and allowing the skirt to drape to floor level.

Starch was first introduced from Holland in 1565 and neck ruffs began to be fashionable for both men and women; as they got larger and more elaborate they acquired wire frames for support.

Men's dress was often more elaborate and colourful than women's. Throughout the period men wore tight leg coverings made of velvet, wool or silk, sometimes worn with a 'cod-piece' to accentuate masculinity. The doublet or 'paltock' tunic, open from the waist up, displayed an elaborately embroidered shirt, and was worn with a cloak in rich cloth with very full sleeves and sometimes a fur collar.

In time this style also developed towards padded shoulders, giving a wide square silhouette, and worn with padded and slashed pantaloons tied in above the knee. The tunic developed into a doublet padded with 'bombast' (rags and bran) or shaped with whalebone to reproduce a protruding paunch then called a 'peasecod belly'.

Over this was worn a 'jerkin', a sleeveless cloak suspended from the shoulders, draping the back to increase the square silhouette effect. Men wore shaped felt hats, some with feathers, their hair often long, but later, when the wearing of carefully trimmed beards came into fashion, the hair was worn shorter.

Shoes ranged from fine leather boots to velvet shoes and wooden 'pattens'. Women's hair was generally hidden, except in front, by a variety of French hoods worn on the back of the head with a tube of fabric hanging at the back.

Gloves were made in many fabrics and often decorated with coloured leather, cut and slashed, and sometimes with gauntlets and fringes.

The poorer people copied these styles when they were able to, but there was a substantial second-hand clothes market, going even to third and fourth hand. Soper Lane (now widened and called Queen Street) had an 'Eve Chipping' which was an evening street market for old clothes. It was popular in the summer months.

Some idea of how a lady expected to be treated may be gathered from an extract from a letter sent to her husband by Lady Elizabeth Compton who eloped in the baker's basket carried by Lord Compton who was by now the Earl of Northampton. She wrote:

My sweet life, I pray and beseech you to grant me, your kind and loving wife, £1,600 and also £600 added

111

yearly for charitable purposes; also I will have three horses for my own saddle that none shall dare to lend or borrow; also I will have two gentlewomen less one be sick but also believe me it is an indecent thing for a gentlewoman to stand momping alone when God hath blessed her Lord and Lady with a great estate. For either of these women I must and will have a horse.

Also I will have six or eight gentlemen and I will have my own coaches, one lined with velvet for myself, and four very fine horses, and a coach for my woman with four good horses.

An Elizabethan gentleman and his wife: he wears a heavily-padded doublet and long hose, the lower part tight-fitting and the upper also heavily padded. She has a loose open gown with a stand-up collar and puff sleeves, round her waist is a long decorated chain and ornament

Luckily the Earl of Northampton was not only very rich he was also very generous. He founded the delightful 'Trinity Hospital' at Greenwich for twelve poor men of Greenwich and eight of Shottisham. Most of the original buildings are still to be seen by application to the Warden. They are now administered by the Mercers' Company.

When his father-in-law, 'Rich Spencer,' died, Compton paid for an impressive funeral at St. Helen's Church Bishopsgate. He provided the tomb and the funeral procession and had 1,000 men dressed in black attending. There were 320 poor men each of whom were presented a basket containing a black gown, 4 lbs of beef, 2 loaves of bread, a bottle of wine, a candle stick, a pound of candles, 2 saucers, 2 spoons, black puddings, a pair of gloves, a dozen points (laces), 2 red herrings, 4 white herrings and 10 eggs.

A typical street

One idea of what daily living conditions were like can be gathered from a description of the 'High Street' of London of this time. This was called 'Westchepe'. The word came from the Anglo-Saxon 'Ceap' meaning market. To go 'Cheping' was to go marketing! Hence the corruption of the word in Chipping Sodbury, an old marketing town. 'Westcheap' was first mentioned as 'Cheapside' about 1510 and has remained Cheapside ever since. The street had been called Westchep to distinguish it from the east market called Eastcheap and this still exists in the City, although its length has since been reduced.

Westchep in the 15th and 16th century was absolutely typical of London. The retail trade went on both on and off the street. A few of the houses were splendid stone or brick buildings, three or four storeys high, but most of them were timber framed, sometimes only one storey high, made of lathe and plaster or brick infilling. In many cases the upper floors were built out several feet from the front and overhung the street beneath. With few exceptions each building had its sign hanging out over the pathway. You can imagine the creaking din these would make on a windy day, quite apart from the danger of the odd one crashing down on the heads of passers-by! Houses were not numbered as they are now, as the sign supplied the address and it would be possible for a letter to be sent to: 'Mr. John Clopton, at the house next door to the Golden Fleece in Westchepe or if he be not there then at the Coney on the Hoop in the Poultrey.'

In the course of time competition made the signs become much bigger, so much so that after the Great Fire in 1666 the City Corporation ordered that all replacements were to be fixed flat on the face of the buildings. The London Museum and the Guildhall Museum have several examples. Visitors to London about this time have remarked on the wide variety of goods on sale in the 'Cheap'. But there were many disturbances. Stall holders

London Bridge: *Nonsuch House is in the centre*

were often inconvenienced by the City authorities moving them off the street to make room for a great procession or for the preparations for a joust to take place. The 'Cheap', therefore, probably attracted more of the itinerant type of stall holder than the other markets with more stable conditions of tenure.

On these occasions the wealth of the merchant occupiers was well displayed by dressing the fronts of the buildings with fine tapestries and rich material, such displays were particularly elaborate on a line of buildings immediately east of St. Mary-le-Bow Church, opposite the Mercers' Hall. This was known as the 'Mercery', and here were the homes of wealthy Goldsmiths and Mercers.

A stone gallery called the 'Crown Silde' had been built by Edward III on the east side of the church, after a previous grandstand had collapsed under Queen Philippa and himself, and remained in use, and Henry VIII and his ladies used it to watch jousts and the annual Midsummer Eve 'March of the Watch'. After the Great Fire when Christopher Wren came to rebuild the church he furnished the tower with a token gallery to commemorate the first one.

Cheapside was lined on both sides under the projecting signs with shops called 'penthouses'; often these were very small with no glazed windows, but had wooden shutters that were taken down each morning. There were some stalls rented out by the City Council. These shacks, or 'selds' as they were called, jutted out into the ill-defined pathway and each had its own accumulation of rubbish and filth. Add to this the clamour of loud-mouthed apprentices, artisans, craftsmen, or journeymen hucksters shouting the details of their wares. The less well-to-do merchants slept on the floors above their shops or, if they were even more poor, they shared the space under the counter with their apprentices. Cheapside was completely destroyed by the Great Fire in 1666 and almost all that is left is the street names.

A Walk around Cheapside

Starting at the east end (at Bank), and moving west-wards, the street was called Poultry because of the Poulterers' stalls which occupied this part of it. The first turning on the right (Northside) is now St. Mildred's Court and in Tudor times led to St. Mildred's Church. At this time it was called Scalding Alley because of the Poulterers' scalding houses situated there. Next we would have come to Comptor Alley leading to the 'Poultrey Comptor', one of the two City gaols in charge of the Sheriffs. This alley ran alongside the 'Rose Tavern' which later became a bookshop.

The next court on the right, now called Grocers' Hall Court, led to an entrance to Grocers' Hall. In Tudor times this was 'Coney Hope' Lane from, as Stow says: 'of old time so called of such a sign of three conies hanging over a poulterer's stall at the Lanes end.' The whole of this frontage on Poultry is now covered by the Midland Bank building. Across the road we see Bucklersbury, the name coming from Thomas Buckerel who lived there in the 13th century. In Snow's time there were the remains of a tenement building on Poultry. This house was called 'The Barge' from which Stow deduced that at one time, before the river Walbrook was built over, barges were rowed up as far as this, and used to tie up alongside the building. Sir Thomas More came to live at this house in 1513 and stayed for 20 years.

The next street on the north side is Old Jewry and led into the area originally occupied by Jews in London. This area went as far as Ironmonger Lane and stretched back northwards nearly to the Guildhall. All Jews were banished from the country by Edward I. In Stow's time on the corner of Old Jewry there was a building which had been built on the site of a Jew's house, and was known as the Old Wardrobe or the King's Palace in Old Jewry. Thomas Becket was born in a house on the corner of Ironmonger Lane about 1118, the site then housed the Chapel of St. Thomas of Acon which stood there in Stow's time. The chapel had a bell which was rung at 6 am in the morning and which was a signal for the City gates to be opened. The Great Bell at St. Martin-le-Grand ringing at night was the signal for the gates to be closed.

The Church of St. Mary Colchurch stood on the other corner of Old Jewry and in 1163 Peter the Chaplain became the Bridge Master and was responsible for building the first stone London Bridge in 1176. This same bridge was used until 1830.

Until 1538 there was a small school in the precinct of St. Thomas of Acon and one of the scholars was John Colet. He became a famous Dean of St. Paul's Cathedral and in 1510 founded St. Paul's School in the Cathedral's churchyard.

Queen Street on the south side of the road was known in Stow's time as Soper Lane and took its name from Allan Lesopar in the time of Edward II. Stow goes on to say:

not from soap making as some have supposed.

I have not read or heard of soap in the City till within this four score years; that John Lane dwelling in Grasse Street set up a boiling house for this city of former time was served of white soap in hard cakes from beyond the seas and of grey soap speckled with white very sweet and good from Bristow (Bristol) sold here for a penny the pound and never above a penny farthing, and black soap for a halfpenny per pound.

King Street on the north side did not come into existence until after the Great Fire in 1666 when Wren created it to provide a grand road entry for Guildhall.

On the corner of Ironmonger Lane stood St. Martin Pomery and behind it and still standing in the lane is the Mercers' Hall.

In this area there are many Tudor street names linked to the market and its commodities.

Honey Lane became a market place in its own right after the Great Fire of London when the City Corporation wanted to clear Cheapside of stalls and moved them into this area. In Stow's time it was the site of two churches—All Hallows and St. Mary Magdalene. Opposite Honey Lane is St. Mary le Bow Church possibly so called because of the 'bowed' arches of the Norman crypt on which it was built and still stands. The 'bows' can also be seen in the design of the belfry. The bells here joined with St. Martin-le-Grand, All Hallows, Barkynge by the Tower, St. Bride, Fleet Street, St. Giles, Cripplegate, to sound the curfew each night.

The Great Bell was also rung at 9 o'clock each night to warn all apprentices that they should be indoors. The church was one of several used for the Archbishop of Canterbury's 'Court of Peculiars', known as the 'Court of Arches'. The name may have come from this association with the church. In the churchyard today we find the statue of a man who was very much of the Elizabethan age—Captain John Smith. He became the first governor of Virginia in 1608 and is remembered because his life was saved by the first Red Indian visitor to this country—Princess Pocahontas. Smith was captured by her father and was about to be executed when she intervened to save his life. She came to this country in 1616 as the wife of Captain John Rolfe, a colleague of Smith, and was very popular at the court of James I. She died on the way home at Gravesend, where she is buried. John Smith is buried at St. Sepulchre's Church in Holborn Viaduct.

Continuing westwards we come to Milk Street on the right and on the opposite side of the road, Bread Street. The next street on the other side of the road, which is now only a footway through the new Bank of England building, was Friday Street. The area between Bread Street and Friday Street, on the south side of Cheapside, was known as 'Goldsmith's Row', and the richness of the goods sold there was admired by the many foreigners who visited London at that time.

Some idea of the quality of Elizabethan goldsmiths' work can be gathered by examining the so-called 'Cheapside Hoard' in the London Museum. It appears to have belonged to a goldsmith and was found in a wooden box under the floor of a building in Cheapside which was being demolished in 1912. The date of the articles has been put at about 1600. Friday Street was the market for non-meat days, and mostly supplied fish.

On the corner of Wood Street on the north side, you can still see the oldest buildings that remain in Cheapside. These were built in 1687, after the Great Fire. They stand on part of the churchyard of 'St. Peter Cheap' or St. Peter Wood Street. Originally this fronted on to Cheapside. Stow says: 'the long shop or shed encroaching on the High Street before this church wall was licenced to be made in the year 1401 yielding to the Chamber of London 30/- and 4d yearly for a time but since 13/- and 4d.'

A Tudor bronze torch-holder made in the shape of a dragon

On the east side of Wood Street stood the second of the City Comptors which had been moved there from Bread Street in 1555. The next turning on the right (Cheapside north side) is Gutter Lane and there seems little doubt that the name comes from 'Godrun' or 'Goderane' who was a tenant here when the Domesday Book was compiled. It has always been the centre for the Saddlers and their rebuilt Hall is there today. Evidence has been found in excavations, of it being used by leather workers from as early as Saxon times. Cheapside had several other adornments; in the centre of the road which may well have been wider than it is today stood the Eleanor Cross erected to the memory of his queen by Edward I. It was destroyed by the Puritans and the only authentic one of these crosses remaining near London is the one at Waltham. East of the Eleanor Cross, opposite the end of Old Jewry, stood the Great Conduit, a lead cistern cased in stone, one of nine built in the City in the 13th century, the water being brought in pipes from the Tyburn river.

Perhaps Cheapside can best be summed up by some lines from 'London Lykpenney' (in London lacking a penny) written by John Lydgate. It tells the story of the countryman up from Kent for a law suit at Westminster, who lost all his money and wandered into the City. He is cried at on all sides to buy, and eventually in Cornhill he is offered his own hood which had been stolen in Westminster. It is clear that the yarns about Petticoat Lane were not new!

> Then to the Cheap I'gan me drawn
> Where much people I saw for to stand
> One offered me velvet, silk and lawn
> Another he taketh me by the hand
> Here is Paris thread, the finest in the land
> Grete chepe of clothe they gan me bete
> Then came there on and cried 'hot shepes fete'
> Rushes fair and grene.

How to Get There

GUY'S HOSPITAL

Address: St.Thomas Street,
                           S.E.1.

By Underground
London Bridge Station (Northern Line, Via Bank)—come
out of station on to Borough High Street and turn left
into St. Thomas Street: the hospital is on the right-hand
side of the street.

By Bus
7, 8a, 10, 13, 21, 35, 40, 43, 47, 133 and 257 across London
Bridge—get off for London Bridge Station and turn into
St. Thomas Street.

The shelter from the old London Bridge is in one of the quadrangles of the Hospital—visitors are usually admitted to it.

SOUTHWARK CATHEDRAL

Address :   London Bridge,
                   S.E.1

By Underground and by Bus
As for Guy's Hospital.
The Cathedral is on the West side of Borough High Street, almost directly opposite London Bridge Station. It is suggested that a visit to Guy's Hospital and a visit to Southwark Cathedral might be combined into one outing. And note Tooley Street, which adjoins Borough High Street on the east side, just to the north of the station.

ALL HALLOWS BARKYNGE BY THE TOWER

Address :   Byward Street,
                   E.C.3

By Underground
Tower Hill (Circle and District Lines)—turn left out of station down path to Byward Street. Turn right along Byward Street. All Hallows is opposite, in the angle between Byward Street and Great Tower Street.

By Bus
Nearest bus routes are the 42 and 78 in the Minories—get off at Tower Bridge and walk along above the Tower to All Hallows; or the 10 and 70 in Fenchurch Street—get off for Mark Lane and walk down Lane to Great Tower Street. Slightly farther away are the buses which cross London Bridge, the 7, 8a, 10, 13, 21, 35, 40, 43, 47, 133 and 257—get off at north side of Bridge and walk to the east through Lower Thames Street, past Billingsgate Market and turning north just past Custom House.

THE TOWER OF LONDON

Address: Tower Hill,
                      E.C.3.

By Underground and Bus
As for All Hallows Barkynge by the Tower.
Tower Hill, the open space to the west of the Tower
faces you as you turn left out of the station.
It is suggested that a visit to the Tower and a visit to
All Hallows might be combined into one outing.

THE TEMPLE CHURCH

Address: Fleet Street,
                      E.C.4.

By Underground
Temple Station (Circle and District)—turn left out of
station and head north via Arundel Street to the Strand.
Turn right in the Strand and continue till it joins Fleet
Street at Temple Bar. (Note in passing St. Clement Danes
Church on your left in the Strand). Continue along Fleet
Street to Inner Temple Lane, turn right into Lane through
the gateway, and follow lane to Church.
Chancery Lane (Central Line)—turn into Chancery Lane
and continue till it joins Fleet Street: Gateway to Inner
Temple Lane is directly opposite. (NB: Chancery Lane
Station is closed on a Sunday. Also, Aldwych Station,
possibly the nearest—turn right out of station, along
Strand and Fleet Street to Inner Temple Lane—is open
only at rush hours.)

By Bus
4a, 6, 9, 11, 13 and 15 run along Fleet Street—get off for
Inner Temple Lane.
109, 177 and 184 run along Victoria Embankment—get
off for Temple. 7, 8, 22, 23 and 25 run along High Holborn
—get off for Chancery Lane.

ST BRIDE'S CHURCH

Address: Fleet Street,
      E.C.4.

By Underground
Blackfriars Station (Circle and District; and Southern
Region)—turn north along New Bridge Street to Ludgate
Circus (with St. Paul's Cathedral up Ludgate Hill on
your right). Turn left at Ludgate Circus into Fleet Street:
the entrance to St. Bride's Church is on your left, beside
the Reuter's building.

By Bus
17, 45, 63, 76, 109, 141, 177 and 184 run across Blackfriars Bridge—get off for Blackfriars or (on 17, 45, 63,
141, plus the 168) at Ludgate Circus. Otherwise, as for
The Temple Church—the two churches might be visited
on one outing.

ST BARTHOLOMEW THE GREAT (Smithfield)
By Underground
Aldersgate (Metropolitan and Circle). (NB: This station
is not open on Sundays.)
Farringdon (Metropolitan and Circle).
St. Paul's (Central).

By Bus
7, 8, 22, 23 and 25 run along Holborn Viaduct—get off
for Giltspur Street.
63, 143 and 221 run along Farringdon Road—get off for
Holborn Viaduct (Charterhouse Street or Long Lane).
4a run along Aldersgate Street—get off for Long Lane.

ST JOHN'S CHURCH (Clerkenwell)

By Underground
Farringdon (Metropolitan and Circle).
Aldersgate (Metropolitan and Circle—Not open on Sundays).

By Bus
5, 170 run along Clerkenwell Road—get off to west of junction with John Street.
63, 143 and 221 run along Farringdon Road—get off for Clerkenwell Road.
4 and 277 run along Goswell Road.
279 runs along St. John Street.

NB. For further details on St. Bartholomew's and St. John's, see suggested walk on page 70.

ST MARY-LE-BOW.
Address:
Cheapside,
E.C.2

By Underground
St. Paul's (Central Line)—from station walk along Cheapside—Church is on the right, just before the junction of Cheapside and Queen Street.
Bank (Central and Northern Line)— from station walk along Poultry until it becomes Cheapside: Church is on the left, just after junction of Cheapside and Queen Street.
Mansion House (Circle and District)—from station follow Queen Victoria Street across Cannon Street till it joins Queen Street; turn left into Queen Street, then left again at junction with Cheapside.

By Bus
7, 8, 22, 23 and 25 run along Poultry and Cheapside.
4 (4a) runs along Aldersgate Street,—get off for St. Paul's, walk along Cheapside.

WESTMINSTER ABBEY (S.W.1.)

By Underground

Westminster (Circle and District)—turn right out of station in Bridge Street and cross square.

St. James's Park (Circle and District)—turn right out of station and walk straight on for Abbey.

By Bus

3, 11, 23, 29, 39, 59, 76, 77, 88, 127, 134, 159, 163 and 168.

Opening hours :	Daily : 8 am—7 pm (6 pm October —March) (On Sundays only the nave and transepts.)
Chamber of the Pyx	Weekdays : 10.30 am—6.30 pm. (4 pm in winter) Admission free.
Norman Undercroft (Abbey Museum)	Weekdays : 10.30 am—4.30 pm (4 pm in winter.) Admission 6d.

The Abbey is open for services only on Ash Wednesday, Good Friday and Christmas Day.

The main entrance to the Abbey is by the West Door, but access to the Chamber of the Pyx and the Norman Undercroft can be gained from Dean's Yard by the South Cloister.